The Effective Entrepreneur

is dedicated to my 'home team' of:

Eileen

Pam   Tim   Chris   Siân

Laura

Andrew   Tom/Ruby   Lucy

Mimi   Michael

every single one a star and, collectively, a brilliant squad.

The Effective Entrepreneur

- A practical guide to leadership and management of others and self

....

Book Design and Setting by Neil Coe (neil@cartadesign.co.uk)

Set in Rotis Serif 10.5 on 13.5pt

First published in 2007 by;

Ecademy Press
6 Woodland Rise, Penryn,
Cornwall UK TR10 8QD
info@ecademy-press.com
www.ecademy-press.com

Printed and Bound by;
Lightning Source in the UK and USA

Printed on acid-free paper from managed forests. This book is printed on demand, so no copies will be remaindered or pulped.

ISBN-978-1-905823-22-2

The Effective Entrepreneur

- A practical guide to leadership and management of others and self

CONTENTS:

4 SELF LEADERSHIP AND MANAGEMENT

5 LEADING AND MANAGING OTHERS

6 IDEAS INTO ACTION

7 A LITTLE HELP FROM YOUR FRIENDS

8 CONCLUSION

i. Why I wrote The Effective Entrepreneur

It was a golden moment. Completing a review of progress at the end of the third quarter, told me that I was again on schedule to achieve all of my annual goals. As those goals covered all aspects of my business and personal lives, that conscious realisation was good news in itself.

Even better, it prompted me to notice and appreciate the great inner feel good factor that I had enjoyed over the previous year or so and which continues today.

The previous three months had seen a couple of 'arrival' points through completed projects. However, the great feeling was not one of completion or arrival but of a great ongoing journey. My satisfaction was derived from making good progress in the way to which I would aspire towards selected destinations of great appeal.

Previously, I had traditionally scored pretty well by external measures, and normally felt very positive about most aspects of my life, but my current sense of well being was reaching new heights and was it all inclusive.

How had this happy state of affairs arisen?

The critical change seemed to have occurred over a short period. Like many 'overnight' successes, it followed a long gestation. In my case, the most obviously relevant parts of my journey had comprised twenty five years of leading my own enterprises and several additional years of observing, advising and supporting other entrepreneurs.

Statistically speaking, the results of companies that I led puts me in the top 1% of entrepreneurs but it never felt entirely that way. Much of my time and energy was spent fighting fires. Persistence, drive and resilience and all the effort and tensions associated with those terms generated the typical flavour of most days.

Circumstances in my companies and their surrounding markets and industries often seemed unprecedented and unstructured. Business theory about anticipating market and industry changes, then organising my business to serve customers to the greatest mutual advantage was far more honoured in the breach than in the observance. Typically, we fought to sell what we already had. Self reliance and independence were more in evidence than close harmonious partnerships with other parties.

Outside work, I have long been blessed with fulfilment through my family and have derived much pleasure from my sporting interests and pursuits. However, when I occasionally stopped to think more expansively, I often felt there must be more to life than I was experiencing yet I neither widened nor deepened my interests in any consistent way,

Following the sale of my largest company in 2001, I carried out a series of assignments as a business consultant and coach – across a range of both growth and recovery situations.

My enjoyment of this pattern of working grew rapidly and I committed to it, rather than returning to run a single enterprise. I evolved my relationships with companies into Chairmanships to reflect my wish to work with compatible teams over a medium term period to build great businesses. Typically, I would also invest, sometimes alongside a Venture Capitalist or other Business Angels.

By 2005/06, I would normally be involved with three or four companies and coaching several Managing Directors on a one-to-one personal basis at any one time.

After five years of the 'pluralist' life, the financial track record of my clients and investees looked pretty good with the current portfolio in good shape and promising some more spectacular outcomes. Just as importantly to me, I was now working enjoyably with and through other people far more than ever before.

Furthermore, I felt much more on 'top of my game' and in control of my time. I was substantively determining my agenda rather than being controlled by 'events' or other people's priorities. In personal life, I was making manifest and satisfying progress across an enhanced range of interests.

What was I doing differently? Could I define the approach I was bringing to entrepreneurial businesses to enable a way above typical proportion of them to deliver stellar results?

These were the circumstances and questions that led me to ponder and then write down my ideas for being an effective business leader. The extension into 'self' leadership and management and focus on 'independent' businesses and business leaders came later, evolving from the emergent responses to my questions.

The motivation to turn the results of my pondering into a published book arose from two related sentiments.

Firstly, and I will not dwell on this one, I have been very lucky in life and that good fortune is reflected in my current circumstances. I am now motivated to help others. If reading my story and ideas sets others on course for their success I would find that deeply satisfying.

There would be some irony in fulfilment of that wish for I do not expect to write anything that has never been written or spoken before. Much of what I will say is my adaptation of sage advice proffered to me in the past – to which I paid precious little attention. It has been a disturbing discovery that the knowledge that now seems most important to business success was available and 'known' by me long before I actually used it. In fact, discovering the profound truth of some old adages left me wondering, "why didn't I listen?" when I had the chance.

Why should you read anything that has been said before? Firstly, it is just possible that certain useful points are, in fact, new to you as I draw on lessons learnt from many experiences and sources. I have been around for a long time. Secondly, my form of words or synthesis of ideas may register with you when previous exposure to the same topics has not. We all relate differently to any particular input and for some of you my expressions will 'strike the chord' that makes the critical difference.

However, the most likely reason that a statement will grab your attention is because it is pertinent to a current need of yours. The human mind has a great ability to filter out the 'noise' of irrelevant messages in order to concentrate on and apply what matters most at any given time. It would be brilliant for both of us if that time is now.

I have written this book on the basis that for many people the time is right for you to utilise what it says. The emphasis in that statement is on 'utilise'. You should expect there to be much that you already 'know' but do not apply. When that is the case, ask yourself, 'Why not? How about starting now?'

My second motivation in this project is simply the challenge of doing it, i.e. to discover for myself if I can write down a single coherent and comprehensive framework that would encapsulate what I do to sustain effective entrepreneurship. Only a practical outcome would have real meaning so that framework will need to be relatively concise. It will need to be read, understood and remembered if it is to have any worth. It will be your conclusion that ultimately matters but I will report back on how I feel that I have met this challenge at the end of the book.

If I can succeed in my mission, the result will be of significant value to independent business leaders. That status, in turns, leads to the glimmer of an entrepreneurial opportunity. I will set up an *'Effective Entrepreneur'* web site to promote dialogue between you, me and our peers[1]. That could turn into a mini business in its own right. That is entrepreneurship in action. I have objectives and returns in mind for my efforts – I can only succeed when I contribute to your goals.

Let us look forward to mutual success.

[1] Access via www.johncaines.com

ii. Why you Should Read It – the Proposition

You now have an idea of how I came to write *The Effective Entrepreneur*. Why should you read it?

Ask yourself if the following proposition is of value to you:

For readers fully engaging with it, this book gives hard working business leaders the opportunity to learn how to achieve full success in their business and personal lives. Unlike many other business writers, I have successfully led independent businesses in good times and bad, so the ideas put forward are practical to implement for other entrepreneurs.

If that proposition offers no value to you, stop now. If it does, consider what that value may be for you.

To obtain your full return from this book, you must promise yourself to read it actively and critically, relating to your own actual practices and performance as you proceed. Allow yourself to feel enjoyment and excitement as you realise how much you are already doing right and as you discover further ideas to enable you to perform even better.

Whether the book's prescriptive aspects work directly for you or not, you still have the opportunity to learn. Please think critically. Whenever you do not readily agree with my views, ask yourself what is the alternative, what is better for you? Either way, when you put your learning into practice you will be on the way to success and fulfilment.

iii. Acknowledgements

As *The Effective Entrepreneur* interprets and reflects all my experiences to date, the candidates for acknowledgement are rather numerous. Extended to its logical conclusion, I need to thank everyone that I have met, or observed in person or through the media, or whose views I have read or to whom I have listened. As such an agglomeration is too wide to be meaningful; I will narrow the field somewhat.

Let me quickly deal with a small group who have contributed invaluably. I have learnt a lot from people whose businesses failed, or who worked in a way that I detested or who let me down. Fortunately, that is a small group and many more are in the positive experience category to which I now turn.

In terms of formal education, the London Business School was clearly the best thing that happened to me. My two year MBA programme transformed my view of the world and opened up avenues that were previously unimaginable to me.

In the event, I took a career path that would have been attainable without going to Business School. How much my MBA studies influenced my subsequent executive and business performance is open to debate. What is incontrovertible and demands my deep gratitude is the whole Business School experience that changed my outlook on life as a whole. It showed me that I could determine my level of success, rather than have others decide it for me. In this respect, it was, inevitably, my fellow students who taught me most, and several of them have continued to provide a life long learning-by-example facility for me. And in truth, graduating from one of world's top business school's gave me a level of self confidence in my ability that may never have emerged without it.

When I consider the value of two great years and the continuing benefits of Business School I must acknowledge and thank Professor David Myddleton who conducted the critical admission interview with me. My personal and academic credentials were raw at best. He must have seen something to rank me ahead of more polished candidates with far superior academic attainments and then exercised the courage to take the unconventional course.

It is people that I have met in business who have given me the most direct insights into what does and does not work. This broad group sub divides into those that I have worked with, those in other organisations with whom I have done business and those where my contact has been limited to observation. There may be ten or twenty individuals who have been most instructive over the three relevant decades. Each version of a list of names that I drafted seemed too long or too short so I am going to keep it anonymous just noting particular thanks to those people who have set out to be helpful to me. By definition, they know who they are.

A slightly different group is those who have 'selected' me without solicitation on my part. Decades of running a business inevitable means decades of pitching for business. Selling has often dominated a great proportion of my time. Intensive campaigns, all too often came to count for nothing through not winning and sometimes the great triumph of another big order could be briefly savoured. Given the often frenetic effort of a major sales pitch and fretful period of waiting for a decision, the occasional phenomena of receiving a 'bluebird' call (i.e. unexpected, out of the air) inviting me to do something new and worthwhile has been very welcome.

'Blubird' calls which have led to changes in direction and significant opportunities have come from Geoff Hester, Terry Harbour, Vic Forrington, Phil Tellwright, Tony Stott, Suzanne Hall-Gibbins and Stephen Shurrock. In succession, their initiatives were instrumental in bringing me away from the corporate world into the entrepreneurial sector, setting me up as an independent business practitioner, introducing me to the burgeoning business opportunities around Information Technology, placing me at the heart of entrepreneurial funding activity in my region, taking up my first Chairmanship of a Venture Capital backed business, establishing my career as a business coach and giving me the opportunity to run a quoted company. I owe them a lot.

Public speaking can be another form of career or business boosting opportunity. People who have taken a chance by inviting me to present at their events include Neilson Kite, Steve Gooding, Michael Howse, Stuart Chapman, Richard Male, Andrea Blakesley, Professor Barry Davies and George Heath. The latter was one of the first and most insistent advocates of me committing my ideas to print so he certainly deserves an extra mention amongst people that have made a difference to me.

Both sets of invitations involved some risk and putting faith in me, as opposed to my company's products or prospects as a financial investment, on something that mattered to the caller. I really appreciated these statements of confidence and did my best to see that they were validated by the results I produced.

In the latter pluralist phase of my career, one big change to my approach to business leadership and life has arisen from the discovery of Coaching. For me, its precepts make a great deal of sense and offer the means to communicate, in both directions, more clearly than I had attained previously. In business, a Coaching approach offers the means to simplify many situations to good effect and gives a structural framework for what I do. Using a coaching philosophy and techniques to leadership and management for others and myself has reaped a rich harvest for me.

Coaching has registered so strongly with me because it is about what I do, as opposed to what a business does, or should do, and it has universal application. Indeed, in business and personal life it leads to aspirations, plans and actions being compelling and comprehensive rather than piecemeal.

Coaching is one of those terms whose meaning has become somewhat elastic as it has become more popular. I give my definition in Chapter 7.2. As part of my training to be a Coach, I gained accreditation in NLP (Neuro Linguistic Programming). I soon found NLP to be consistent with, and make sense of, my experiences in the past. NLP concepts and techniques have become fundamental to the way I lead and manage myself and interact with others. David Shephard taught me NLP and I thank and recommend him.

When it came to putting pen to paper for *The Effective Entrepreneur*, I benefited enormously from expert help. Mindy Gibbins-Klein turned a vague idea into a structured landscape with clear path through it. She took me from staring at an unclimbable mountain of undefined work to a manageable project with clear bite-sized steps. Mindy really lives up her epithet of 'The Book Midwife'. I want to thank her publicly for her exceptional service and to recommend her to any reader who needs to get a book out of their system.

After six months of working with Mindy and my keyboard, there was the daunting moment when somebody else had to see my work. Fortunately, it was a group of friends whom I knew would give me the frank and constructive feedback that I would need to make *The Effective Entrepreneur* suitable for a wider audience or, conceivably, to tell me that it should head for the waste paper basket.

My reviewers did sterling work and everything they told me was much appreciated whether or not specific ideas made it into the much revised version now in your hands. That group to whom I also extend my thanks comprised Neilson Kite, Peter Beech-Allan, Diane Savory, Rob Nicoll and Tony Burgess. Tony is an outstanding Coach who made the introduction to Mindy so I owe him a lot on more than one count. Diane and Rob both run independent businesses and both kindly told me that I seemed to have been writing to them personally. That was the greatest encouragement to keep going despite my doubts and the daunting amount of rework that was all too obviously necessary.

On a personal basis, I can speak with conviction about the self leadership and self management processes that are central to this book as I have practised them myself. They enabled me to feel much more on top of my game, in control of my time and progressing towards bigger goals than ever before. For a while, *The Effective Entrepreneur* blew that claim sky high. Unlike other things that I do, it was very difficult to predict any relationship between input time and output. It also had to be 100% finished before it had any value for anyone but me. That meant I was susceptible to that 'last 5% of the project needing 50% of the time syndrome' which had so often made me very impatient as I waited for software developers or builders to complete their work.

Whilst writing this book, there were periods when I was certainly no longer on top of my time management. I found myself snatching too many early mornings and late evenings to stay even close to my production schedule. That way of working must have been very frustrating for my family and a throw back to earlier years when, like many entrepreneurs, my work displaced far too much of the time and attention that they deserved. This book is dedicated to them; they know that the great appreciation for their patience and support during this project is just a microcosm of how I feel about them and what they have done for me overall.

Looking ahead, I expect to continue to benefit from my longstanding sources of support, personal development and inspiration. By reading *The Effective Entrepreneur*, you are recruited to that group. Thank you for your custom and, in anticipation, for your feedback.

INTRODUCTIONS

1.1 Leaders, Managers and Entrepreneurs

Many Entrepreneurs have a great vision yet fail to build a successful business because they lack the ability or inclination to turn their big ideas into viable business plans and deliver against them. In other words, they lack the 'ability to execute'.

'Ability to execute' is the hallmark of a good manager. Good Managers deliver what they commit to deliver.

Good management alone will not achieve great things. Creativity and vision are needed to set the goals and direction in the first place.

The ability to envisage a desirable outcome, or Goal, is the starting point of Leadership. To become effective the Leader must then be able to define the Goal precisely and communicate it clearly to the Managers.

Spotting an opportunity that others cannot see is the hallmark of an Entrepreneur. Translating it into a Vision, then to a well defined Goal and communicating it clearly to others who have the ability to execute (i.e. good Managers) is the path to effective Entrepreneurship.

Clear communication of a Goal is not quite enough. The Leader/Entrepreneur must also find the means to motivate others and him or herself to commit fully to its achievement.

The effective Leader will also find the resources to manage effectively – whether from within him or herself or through others.

This book is about how to join Leadership and Management together with the right mix of resources that are aligned and motivated to meet Entrepreneurial Goals.

1.2 About You

You are a leader or aspirant leader of an independent business.

The word 'entrepreneur' is used for convenience rather than to restrict the message to leaders of OMB's (Owner Managed Businesses). An entrepreneur may operate in many settings beyond running his or her own independent business. Examples of other cases could include leading an autonomous unit within a corporate organisation, a project or a voluntary activity. This book generally uses language and cases that are geared to the 'classic' OMB leader but applies to any of the above roles too.

You are a leader building something where you need a team to help you deliver. For the leader, particularly one who is asking for extraordinary results, the need to work with, to motivate and manage others, is often the most difficult challenge. Successfully working with and through other people is, nevertheless, essential if meaningful business Goals are to be accomplished.

You intend to be more than just a manager of a pre-defined operation confined to merely sustaining an established operation, e.g. a departmental function in a large organisation or running a small retail store. Successful companies, economies and societies need a blend of people ready to run today's mature organisations superbly well and another group, including you, who are ever seeking to break out of the *status quo* to improve the lot of themselves and others.

You are less than content with aspects of your current business status, performance and/or personal fulfilment. The reason may be clear in your mind or muddled; you may even be doing fantastically well by all external standards but you just FEEL that you are not as successful as you could or should be.

Your central desire and mission is to lead your team towards something significantly different and better. That better future may or may not be mapped out now – but you are definitely NOT about just managing the *status quo*.

You assume that **it is your role to lead** and you are acting upon that assumption. You have risen to the ancient challenge of **"If not me, WHO? If not now, WHEN?"**

You know that achievement of significant **success in your life needs action** on your part. It is more than a dream; you are not relying on riches via a lottery ticket or inheritance; you are going to create it.

You may already be working towards a set goal. You may just have an ill defined 'away from' restlessness such as wanting to escape the boredom, restrictions or just plain lack of spending power that frustrate you today. Whether your initial driving force is 'towards' or 'away from', the thoughts and techniques of *The Effective Entrepreneur* are equally applicable.

1.3 About this Book

The core of *The Effective Entrepreneur* is presented in four distinctive sections to meet the challenge of delivering its ambitious proposition to you.

The first section sets out some foundation blocks with some fundamental ideas that underpin both thinking about and actual engagement in entrepreneurship. As such, they also set the tone and provide underlying themes that run throughout the book.

"It's a wise man that learns from the mistakes of others." It is certainly less expensive that making them yourself, so in the second section, an autobiographical selection of my less good decisions and actions are mixed in with descriptions of better judgement and execution. These examples are offered for your consideration. Because of your different and fresh perspective on my narrative, you will also derive additional lessons that I still have not discerned.

When writing this section, it was interesting and meaningful for me to note how many lessons have been learnt in retrospect rather then being realised and applied at the time. Improving the ratio towards less retrospective learning would have considerable value and I make specific proposals in this regard in the final section of this book.

Thirdly, I filter and assemble the accumulated lessons of direct personal experience, my interpretation of other ideas and observation of other practitioners into a general framework to show what makes an entrepreneur effective.

In the fourth section, I become directly prescriptive about sound practical processes that take your ideas and turn them into the basis for action.

In my concluding remarks, I bring these approaches together with recommendations that reinforce and support your motivation to implement what you have learned from *The Effective Entrepreneur.*

1.4 About Me

The introductory description 'About You' is also a good description of me so I feel greatly empathetic towards you.

I demonstrated the impatience often associated with entrepreneurs by leaving school as quickly as possible and starting work at sixteen years of age. For six largely unsatisfactory years, I worked in large companies qualifying as an accountant before embarking on a life changing MBA at the London Business School.

For the subsequent thirty five years I have been immersed in independent entrepreneurial businesses. For most of that time, I have been leading my own businesses. Between 1975 and 1989 I evolved from working alone as an independent consultant to leading a successful software company employing seventy five people. In 1990, I disposed of the great majority of that business and kept a unit with eight staff. Over the next eight years, I built it into a profitable group employing five hundred staff across eight countries.

Self determination and self reliance were central to my leadership of companies over some twenty five years. Although these are good and necessary traits, I can now see that I could have worked much more smartly. In my 'career' sheer coalface effort and determination have often been more obvious than incisive strategy and understanding of others. More precise goal setting, greater people orientation and more directness and openness would have made me more effective and less pressurised.

More recently, in the 'portfolio' phase of my career I worked with dozens of owner managed and venture capital backed companies as a Non Executive Chairman or Director, Investor, Coach and Consultant.

From this perspective, it has become clear that I was not alone in making entrepreneurial life difficult for myself. Many business leaders are working incredibly hard under great pressure. Sadly, it is too often true that their strategies can never succeed and leadership performance is just not good enough for them to ever flourish. Often they 'cannot see the wood for the trees', often they are haphazard in their methods and often the managers that report to them do not understand their brief or are simply not good enough themselves. When I have worked with those business leaders to remedy those deficiencies, applying the methods described in *The Effective Entrepreneur* has produced a high ratio of success stories.

Through directly experiencing and observing what does and does not work in business leadership, I believe that I have now evolved an approach that results in effectiveness, less stress and more enjoyment for business leaders. The ideas and methods that I have successfully applied with others are what I would now like to share with you.

FOUNDATION BLOCKS

'Having effected some personal introductions, it is time to get under way with some fundamental ideas about our subject matter. The base level building blocks below will set the reader's mind and give a context for topics raised in later sections.

2.1 Ingredients of Effective Entrepreneurship

Enhancement of one's entrepreneurial or independent business leadership performance is an 'elephant' task, i.e. one that is best tackled by breaking it down into bite sized chunks. The following paragraphs are one way of summarising the ingredients of a recipe for successful entrepreneurship:

Driving Ambition:

Moving beyond dreams and contemplation to taking action must emanate from you. External resources can enhance, channel and add skills and knowledge but the initial desire can only turn into sustained action when it is consistent with your inner core. Let us call this 'big picture' motivation that drives and underpins everything else Driving Ambition.

Skills:

Some combination of skills in a particular market, industry or activity is clearly needed to apply to the particular venture being led by the entrepreneur. This aspect may be the 'something special' referred to below.

There will a set of more generic skills too, including the need to lead and manage people and very probably a degree of personal selling ability too. Priority skills are discussed in Chapter 5.1.

Processes:

Sustaining any successful activity implies that definable repeatable processes are being followed. That requirement applies to an individual steering and conducting his or her own affairs and certainly if other people are to be involved in a coherent way. Chapter 5 describes leadership and management processes with universal application. Explicit consideration of the way you work today against these yardsticks in these everyday activities is a prerequisite to improving performance.

Knowledge:

Knowing your territory in terms of markets, suppliers, competitors and more; knowing the properties and benefits of your product or service and how best to produce, source and deliver, are obvious requirements for the business person.

Often this knowledge is held in a highly unstructured way. It is enormously helpful for yourself - and even more in communication with others - to organise it into a relevant structure. A 'Map' of the eco system of goods and services flowing from 'upstream' through your business to the final customer is particularly helpful. Pictures of your market and industry depicting meaningful sub sectors is both useful and a good test of your knowledge of your landscape. These views together with clear goals are highly conducive to creative and good decision making. Chapter 5.2.3 about Alignment offers useful pointers in this respect.

Knowledge can be gained in many ways and time taken out to update it will pay off handsomely. 'The Value of Perspective', discussed in Chapter 2.4 below, includes a vivid illustration of how knowledge gained from a change in Perspective directly steered an enterprise away from its course towards inevitable failure and back towards viability and its chosen Goal.

Experience is a great source of knowledge. One's own direct experience is an expensive and necessarily limited form of gaining knowledge. 'Learning from My Story' in Chapter 3 is an opportunity to learn from the experience of others, in this case, me. There are innumerable other publications and events from which to gain knowledge from others. Making some time to utilise them is a good investment.

Attitudes

All the skills and knowledge in the world are not enough to guarantee that an individual will be an effective business leader. The right attitudes are even more important. Exactly what constitutes the 'right' attitudes will vary but confidence in one's own ability and belief that one's chosen goals are the right ones and attainable are ever present ingredients of the successful person. Appropriate attitudes and remedying shortfalls are discussed in Chapter 4.2.

Something Special

All discussion of what makes an entrepreneur effective is entirely valid yet revolves around one critical 'mystery' factor.

Sustained success means people continuing to want to do business with you rather than anyone else. There has to be 'something special' around which all else is based. It could be based on product or service innovation, it could be the ability to transfer ideas from one market to sell in another, it could be attaining the very highest levels of trading skills, leadership, customer service and/or sheer determination.

This is the only ingredient that is not developed in later chapters for it is as unique as you and your business.

Action

A specific manifestation of the right attitudes is getting started. Far more people dream about running their own business or similar ambitions than actually do something about it. If you are to be one of the minority who are going to be effective, then you should start immediately you have absorbed this book!

Effective Help

Being independently minded does not mean having to do everything yourself. In fact, that would be a distinctly ineffectual thing to do. Remaining conscious of your leadership, you should employ the very best team of managers you can find and the very best advisers.

You need a clear mind to concentrate on what you do best – and you want assurance that all agreed actions by others will be completed on time to the highest standards. Why would you want it otherwise? Yet many act as though they do by recruiting at minimum cost rather than maximum quality, selecting people who appear easy to manage or continuing to employ non performers.

Sustained Motivation:

We come full circle to motivation or the application of Driving Ambition. The true entrepreneur takes the first step to get started, remains resilient through the difficulties that will inevitably emerge and retains the drive to do his/her very best through good times (when it is easy to slacken off) and bad. It all starts, and only starts, when the next step is taken.

Awareness of this set of ingredients is the first step towards improving performance. For an individual each ingredient can be upgraded either by ourselves or by using a third party.... when there is enough basic motivation to take the first step.

2.2 Begin with the End in Mind

It is often tempting to plough straight into activity, especially one that we enjoy. It is easy to become busy before knowing exactly what we want to achieve and/or the best strategy for getting there. In contrast, applying the adage 'begin with the end in mind' saves much wasted effort in execution and disappointment with actual outcomes.

For any serious endeavour, it is important to know exactly what your required outcome will look like and be seriously motivated to achieve it. When you have that precise knowledge, you will be drawn to that Goal during planning and execution; you will repel any deviations from the course that will take you there.

Whether it is a project, your business, reading this book or the next phase of your life, your success requires you to know at conscious, and fully accept at unconscious, levels what the outcome will be and how it will look, sound and feel when you have accomplished it.

In logical terms, a Goal needs to be well defined to allow planning and execution as logical processes as described in Chapter 5. In emotional or psychological terms a Goal needs to be both motivational and aligned with the 'inner you'. That alignment must include both the confidence that you have the ability to execute your strategy and complete comfort that the result is exactly what you want.

2.2.1 Begin with the End in Mind for Your business

Your business is a central part of your life so let us start with a few comments about its end game or probably more accurately the end of your involvement with it. The longevity of your engagement with it is a fundamental decision.

What is the end date of your involvement? What will the business look like when you depart? How much money do you want to earn from it?" Precise answers create a Well Formed Goal[2], which in turn allows development of a meaningful strategy.

In practice, first responses to these questions are often along the lines of "I don't know. I want to maximise its potential." Vagueness may be understandable but it is most unhelpful. If a well formed goal for your exit cannot yet be formed, introduce an interim date as your practical planning horizon. **If you cannot define what you want at particular time horizon, then shorten it.**

For your interim date, define exactly how the business will look - and it is perfectly ok to add a tag line something like 'and with forward momentum' to remind yourselves and others that it needs to be in good shape to carry on developing beyond that date. Make the most meaningful statement possible about the ultimate outcome too and you will have a useful picture to carry into your planning and doing stages.

Creating an interim step to a long term goal

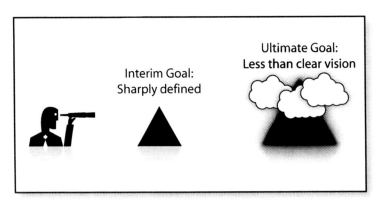

When you have arrived at the planning horizon you set today, time will have passed and you will be able to look ahead more clearly towards your ultimate vision.

---

2 As defined in 2.3 below.

Ultimate Goal:
Vision now clear

Your exit will eventually feature in your specific plans and it is much better to quantify your financial goal as opposed to a phrase like 'maximising its potential'. A set goal does not stop you accepting tactical opportunities to improve your result. The problem with a less specific approach is never knowing when you have reached the point when you should say 'yes' and close negotiations. I have seen several entrepreneurs come to regret rejecting large offers for their businesses, as valuations, and even the viability of any sale, have a nasty habit of disappearing very quickly if markets turn against them.

Emphasising the case for exit date and value to be sharply defined does not imply any lack of interest in what happens to your business beyond that planning horizon. It is important to look beyond and run the business to keep running strongly through and beyond the 'finishing tape'. There are multiple reasons for this insistence:

- You cannot be precise on timing. External events, from stock market crashes to natural or man made disasters, can kill the market so you need the staying power to continue until a propitious time for selling a company. Anyone involved in buying, selling or investing around the dot.com boom can tell you that.

  Staying power is also essential once you are into negotiations with a specific party right up to the point of completion. If a buyer senses that its target will run out of cash or hit other big problems, without the deal being done, you should assume that this weakness will be ruthlessly exploited.

• Secondly, what are the chances of your business being in great shape and commanding a strategic premium price unless it still has strength and obvious growth prospects going forward under new ownership? No buyer will pay a good price for a business that is going nowhere. A business with good growth prospects will earn the best price.

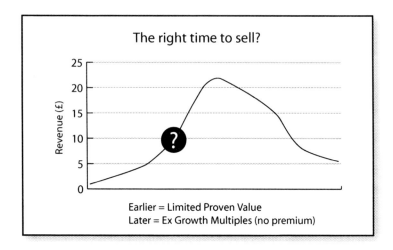

The right time to sell?

Earlier = Limited Proven Value
Later = Ex Growth Multiples (no premium)

• If you are currently indispensable to your business, you may have a problem. New owners must be able to manage their acquisition. You must anticipate this requirement and have a good answer for them.

Those reasons for looking beyond the finishing tape are financial. Finally, look beyond the money to your own requirements at the end of your association with your business. Do you want yourself and others to know you built a great business and left it in great shape or just did ok for yourself and took the money?

2.2.2 Begin with the End in Mind for The Whole You

The date of your exit from your business cannot be considered in isolation. Does commitment to your business exclude all other aspects of your life from your stated Goals and **while you are on the journey?** For most of us, business cannot be the exclusive interest and so later sections of this book will offer the means to incorporate the personal dimensions of your life in both your goal setting and your strategy.

Think of 'the End' as being the outcome at any stage that matters to you rather just the final result at the end of your planning horizon. Evaluate what you want and, if need be, how you truly feel about the balance of sacrifice at one stage and rich rewards at another.

If your business is currently worth being the complete or dominant aspect of your life, it is highly probable that you will eventually have a different dilemma when you leave it. How will it be replaced? I have seen many bored and frustrated retired business people searching for pastimes and identity. If you love what you do, think very hard before taking a payout to leave it too early. It may be irreplaceable until much later in your life.

Conversely, it may be that you really are only in business for the money. If the activity itself gives you less than 100% fulfillment but the money is important enough to keep doing it even though there is something else you would rather be doing then:

- ration your time to allow other preferred activities as you go

- be sure you work long enough only to reaching 'enough' (money) at a set date and

- raise your morale with the conscious thought that this dedication to earning money is the means to enjoy the rest of your time whether in parallel with, or subsequent to, running your business. In this case, you should definitely think about rationing the time that you work for this money.

What role does your business play in your life – what else is important to you in your ideal world? Is the time and priority you give your business activities consistent with that ideal?

2.2.3 Begin with the end in Mind for Other People

Nobody lives in a vacuum. To some extent, other people will matter to everyone, of us hopefully on a voluntary basis although there may be other important relationships that matter too.

Here is one way of developing a map of those thoughts and your perceptions of them:

Mapping Your Relationships				
Category	Names/Sub Groups	What you want from them	What they want from you	Importance
Your partner				
Family				
Friends				
Interest Groups				
Your Community				

Define the main headings as you wish. 'Your Community' could stretch from your neighbourhood through national to global dimensions. It's who and what matters to you.

Your personal or 'life' partner is of course a special case. In the 1970's, research carried out on married couples where at least one spouse held an executive or professional job classified each partner by their level of personal drive and emotional self sufficiency.

Personal Drive	Achievement		
		Involved	Thrusting
		Caring	Loners
	Laid back		
		Needs others - Autonomy	
	Emotional Self Sufficiency		

No single 'right' combination of relationships between spouses emerged. All permutations can work well when they are worked on ... and 'worked on' must ultimately mean 'work with' – *think about it.*[3]

The ideas around that study lead on to more general consideration of the 'what you want' and 'what they want' columns. Do you know? Let me add two ideas for working out the answers:

Firstly, there is the idea of Perceptual Positioning, an NLP[4] technique in which you enhance your effectiveness by improving your understanding of how another party may be seeing a situation and therefore how they may feel and act. Perceptual Positioning is particularly valuable when dialogue is at or approaching stalemate and in preparing for any set of complex negotiations. Almost every NLP guide, of which there are many, will include a description of the process.

3 Charles Handy, *The Elephant and the Flea*, (Random House, 2002)
4 NLP is the acronym for Neuro Linguistic Programming which is more fully explained in Chapter 4.2.

Secondly on the subject of working with the other party about what they want from you, *talk with the other party and ask them!* In personal relationships, it is amazing how often things have gone wrong because of a lack of communication and false assumptions being made even where there is an intention to do the right thing.

Draw up your own table of personal relationships – it's ok to extend my template by the addition of an Action column!

These ideas are important in business terms too. You can use the same sort of table for business relationships but I would suggest making a second separate table as we don't want to deflect focus from our central theme – the inclusion of the non-business people that are important to us. We will return to alignment of business relationships as an important topic in the priority concerns of a business leader.

Measurable business success is rarely the means to total personal fulfilment although for many it will be a major contributor to how we feel about ourselves. Only you will know what and who else matter to you. Why not reflect who and what is important to you in what you actually do?

Perceptual Positioning[5]

One of the first things we learn about the world is that not everyone shares our point of view. To understand a situation fully, you need to take different perspectives, just as when looking at an object from different angles to see its breadth, height and depth. One point of view only gives a single dimension, a single perspective; true from that angle but an incomplete picture of the whole object.

There is no 'correct' perspective in any situation. You build understanding from many perspectives. All are partially true and all are limited. NLP supplies three of these perspectives.

First position is your own reality, your own view of any situation. Personal mastery comes from a strong first position. You need to know yourself and your values to be an effective role model and influence others by example.

---

[5] This description is drawn from Joseph O'Connor's *NLP Handbook*, (Thorsons, 2001).

Second position is making a creative leap of imagination to understand the world from another person's perspective, to think in the way that they think. Second position is the basis of empathy and rapport. It gives us the ability to appreciate other people's feelings.

There are two types of second position:

An **Emotional** second position is about understanding the other person's emotions. You therefore do not want to hurt them because you can imagine their pain.

An **Intellectual** second position is the ability to understand how another person thinks, the kind of ideas they have and the sort of opinions and outcomes they hold.

Third position is a step outside your view and the other person's view to a detached perspective. There you can see the relationship between the two viewpoints. Third position is important when you check the ecology of your outcomes. You have to forget your required outcome for a moment, and look at it in a more detached way to ascertain what works best for both parties.

All positions are useful. The best understanding comes from all three.

Perceptual positions are fundamental tools in the context of resolving relationship problems and in negotiations too. In these situations, knowing your position and another person's position, without necessarily agreeing with it, maximises your prospects of achieving what you want.

2.3 Well Formed Outcomes and Goals

This book frequently refers to Outcomes and Goals, using the terms interchangeably whenever used in the future tense. Knowing where we want to go in the form of required Outcomes and Goals is a cornerstone element for planning and then taking action towards a satisfactory future for ourselves.

Usage and full meaning of these terms will evolve over the following chapters. For now, it is helpful to recall the well known acronym SMART as a good working definition. It has a number of slight variations, which can be used to provide a more comprehensive set of requirements for effective well formed goal setting:

S - **Specific**, significant, stretching

M - **Measurable**, meaningful, motivational

A - **Agreed upon**, attainable, achievable, acceptable, action-oriented

R - **Realistic**, relevant, reasonable, rewarding, results-oriented

T - **Time-based**, timely, tangible, can be tracked

How do you think the following statements measure up to a SMART goal?

"I want to fulfil my potential/ the potential of this business"

It's not enough; it's neither Specific, Measurable nor Time based. We will need to interpret this into a more concrete statement that will represent 'potential' in a SMART way or at least define an interim goal on the way to that end.

"I want to get away from the poverty/boredom/etc that goes with this job".

Ok as a starting point but needs to become specific and timed. When making that conversion it is more psychologically sound to express in positive "towards" (as opposed to "away from") terms.

A world ranked athlete's commitment *"to win the Marathon at the next Olympics"* is a very SMART goal that allows a matching strategy to be produced and then monitored against interim milestones.

To break away from the *status quo*, a defining requirement for readers of this book, we need to know where we would prefer to be. If we are going to do something about it, we must know very precisely what 'it' is. To be actionable and effective, we must translate our dreams into specific outcomes. Our discontent with the *status quo* requires us to set SMART Goals.

2.4 The Value of Perspective

In the panel below, I retell a story from Stephen's Covey's 'Seven Habits of Highly Effective People'[6]. He used it to illustrate the difference between management and leadership.

It also serves wonderfully well in underscoring how easy it is to busily work on the wrong things and head in the wrong direction because you lack a clear picture of where you are heading compared to where you want to go. In contrast, an appropriate view of the landscape, where we are now, our objective and the terrain we have to cover to reach it renders the need to adjust obvious and corrective action easy to identify.

'Wrong Jungle' – A story about (i) Leadership vs. Managing and (ii) Perspective

A group of explorers set out to search for a lost city reputed to have vast storerooms stacked full of gold. They paddled upstream along a great river as far as it would take them knowing they would eventually have to leave the water and travel through thick jungle to the base of a mountain range where the legendary city was sited.

After several days travel, they reached the point where they had to disembark and prepare for the arduous trip overland. They unloaded the canoes and reassembled their supplies for onward transport. Various carrying frames were constructed to give additional capacity and eventually everything was repacked and allocated to the team of local porters. After an overnight stay and then a few more hours' preparation they were ready to continue. There was thick undergrowth to negotiate and so machetes were issued to selected personnel to hack a clear path for the whole expedition. The party was organised into teams, each with an individual responsible for its people, equipment, supplies, and allocated responsibilities to contribute to the overall effort.

The trek got under way. Progress was very slow at first. This was a new experience for most of the travellers and it took some time to pick up the best techniques for cutting a path and then finding the best sequence of men and materials to progress through the bottlenecks. Some of the supplies and equipment were offloaded and repacked into smaller bundles

---

6 Stephen R. Covey, *The 7 Habits of Highly Effective People*, (Fireside, 1989)

as the realities of the harsh environment became all too clear. Eventually these teething problems were solved and the whole party, especially the team leaders, began to feel better as they got some momentum into their forward progress.

At this stage the leader of the whole party decided he should get a better fix on how far the party had already covered and how far there was to go. He climbed a tree to use as a look out point for this purpose. When he arrived at his look out point, he did not like what he saw. The expedition had progressively veered off its course until it was traveling away from the landmark mountaintop that represented their target by about 45 degrees. He called out to the teams below 'Stop, we're heading for the wrong jungle.'

They carried on, nobody heard him – they were too buried in doing what managers do best ... supervising their bit of the organisation, monitoring progress and people and the good ones looking for further gains in their effectiveness of their team. However, the entire business is heading in the wrong direction!

'WRONG JUNGLE!' bellowed the leader 'STOP! We have to change direction.' This time the expedition did hear and stop. From his treetop position, the leader could now assess the correct direction for his goal and re-plan the expedition's next moves.

Managers in many businesses are working hard as 'busy fools' on activities that do not align with the realities of the outside world. The Leader should already have clearly set Goals for the business. Once activities are under way, the Leader's second input is to take a realistic look at what is actually happening and where today's activities will lead. In most businesses, the Leader has a managing or 'doing' role too, so it takes awareness and resolve to step up from that level to the 'treetop'.

Once at the treetop, if a mismatch becomes apparent, the third responsibility and test of leadership is to make the team stop what they are doing and redirect their efforts towards the Goal.

In Covey's story, the Goal is very clear. It is also apparent that the floor of the jungle is no place to assess progress or direction; the big picture is obscured. The leader has to 'climb the tree' and look out at the landscape and the goal to assess if his team is still heading in the right direction.

Whenever you are feeling pressured or too busy, recall and act on the image of Covey's Jungle story. If it is a struggle to persuade your team or clients that they need to stop what they are doing and redirect their efforts, tell them the story and ask them to join you at the 'top of the tree.' A tree top view usually means that shared understanding arrives pretty quickly.

Personally, I like to stretch the metaphor and imagine that the leader also sees some physical hazards like ravines or marshes and some threatening human factor like hostile tribes or an ambush ahead in the middle distance somewhere ahead of the team and in the path to its destination.

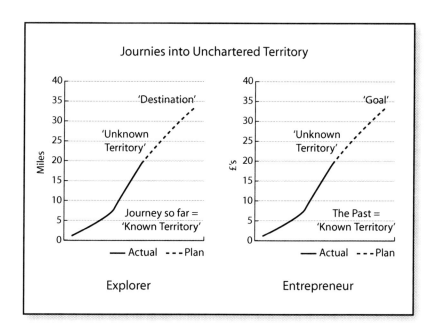

You can relate that fictional picture to business 'road blocks' and competitive actions and use the imagery to good effect. When I am sitting as a Non Executive Director or coach, I often encourage a Chief Executive to get away from managerial level noise and 'climb the tree' to gain a proper perspective. For a business adviser to a growing business, the task is often to help the CEO anticipate the nature of territory into which he/she has never traveled before.

2.5 Successful People...... Act 'As If'

Successful people ACT as if now is the right time, they know everything they need to know, and act with certainty of success[7].

The 'Act As If' phrase is key in this context, for any logical person knows that there is risk, uncertainty and a lack of complete knowledge in any given situation.

Logical unsuccessful people let those factors stop them taking action.

Logical successful people more readily reach the point when they perceive the case for acting on what they know to outweigh those shortfalls.

Once a challenge has been accepted and a route to its achievement formulated, any continuing sense of uncertainty can only act as drag on performance. The best performers have the distinctive ability to 'call' the right time impeccably and act decisively without such doubts.

The successful leader has a bias for action. This is a practical book so do not expect 'proof' of each point made, for that would be neither efficient nor even desirable. It will be much more effective for you to read the text, proactively and critically, absorbing useful points that seem true and relevant, discounting others and moving on. The amalgam of the most relevant points, added to your existing knowledge and applied in your context, will produce your positive pay off.

---

[7] David Shephard, The Performance Partnership Limited summarising a key learning point from NLP.

LEARNING FROM MY STORY

"Fools learn from their own mistakes; it's a wise man that learns from the mistakes of others" (Chaucer)

"History doesn't repeat itself but it does rhyme" (Mark Twain)

Observing how another person handles a situation may usefully illustrate good or bad practice and steer you away from making errors in a similar situation. It is much less expensive than 'learning through doing.' Learning only from your direct experiences puts you at the start of the learning curve in every new situation, which inevitably increases the chance of poor decision making and execution until you evolve the right way of doing things. In business, that evolution may be too long and costly to be viable.

From that belief, I'm going to recall something of my personal story, pointing to specific lessons that I have picked up along the way. This narrative is based on what I have experienced and observed over several decades in the fray of entrepreneurial business. Most of that time has been spent in the driving seat of my own businesses with the balance offering a very good view of the driver of someone else's business.

3.1 Heading Nowhere

Running my own business, building any particular career or even having a career were not in my thoughts until I had been working for a few years. The immediate consequence was drifting around on a random journey.

One must have a truly internalised well defined ambition to ensure success. Without the motivation to act towards a goal, your chances of success are low and the shape of any success is governed by events that happen to you, rather than a drive towards your ideal.

There is no specified starting point for Business Leaders in general and Entrepreneurs in particular. The only prerequisites are the inner drive to do it and taking the next step.

If you have a strong inner drive to become a successful entrepreneur or business leader you can achieve your ambition regardless of your starting point.

To the extent that meeting your ambition requires extra skills or knowledge, these can be obtained.

To the extent that your behaviour needs to be modified, it can be modified.

Feelings and beliefs can get in the way of ambition and performance. They can be modified too, although not without limit. (You must supply the innermost spark of entrepreneurial spirit).

Whatever your current position you can only move towards your goal by taking action.

External assistance is available to bolster your resources to the appropriate level in respect of skills, knowledge, behavioural traits and inhibiting feelings and beliefs.

You only move nearer your Goal by taking the next step – and only you can do that.

In my case, the inner drive was latent for some time until circumstances presented me with the opportunity to 'do my own thing'. When you know what you want you can create those circumstances rather than knowingly or unknowingly waiting for them to occur.

3.1.1 Early days

Until my early twenties, I had no goals, no vision of what I wanted to achieve or what I wanted to become. I lived for today. I mostly enjoyed myself but was readily bored and impatient to move on to the next thing in study and early employment. I was an energetic person with no career or other sustained outlet for my energies.

At my grammar school, I was an obnoxiously rebellious, angry, non-studying ("why should I?") pupil and that condition lasted through to my premature departure still aged fifteen. Only a dedication to playing football and a residual adherence to values and standards of behaviour from my earlier upbringing prevented me going 'off the rails' in a much more serious way.

There was no role model and no information from adults or 'the system' to inspire me towards any positive goals. Neither was my social network going to provide it, for my peers were similarly disconnected from respectable ambition – and mostly respectability or ambition of any sort.

Plainly, with no idea of where I wanted to go, I was going nowhere. My energy had no constructive outlet beyond the football pitch.

How will energy be used?

	Low	High
High	Frenetic but aiming for wrong Goal Or Trouble Maker	Committed and aligned to Goal
Low	'Living Dead' A waste of money	No trouble but Ineffective

Energy Level

Sense of Direction/Affiliation

3.1.2 The Salaried Years

If the above description of me as school leaver gives you the idea of a wildly anarchistic teenager about to run amok, stand by for a shock. I accepted that I needed to work and didn't resist the idea. I got my very long hair cut to an office clerk's 'short back and sides' and applied to work in the National Provincial bank. While I waited for that process to complete I took a temporary job with several of my mates on a production line in a local electronics factory. It was mind-numbingly boring so when I heard that National Provincial didn't want me I jumped at the opportunity that a young Personnel Officer put my way to become a trainee cost accountant. (Who was he? Why did he pick me? We'd had no contact beyond cursory form filling when I signed up for the production line.) I had no idea what an accountant did, but it was different and a job in the offices seemed a move up in my known universe at that time and too good to turn down.

Hands up, I admit it, I enjoyed my early days in the cost accounting department and studying to become a qualified Cost and Works Accountant through day release and night school at the local technical college. Playing plenty of football, a hectic social life and the novelty of being treated as an adult was enough to make me happy, for I was by no means a career minded person yet.

The novelty wore off quickly enough but I persisted with the accounting route and got a big uplift in intrinsic job interest when I moved away to Gloucester to join a 200 employee engineering company to be Assistant Cost Accountant. Leaving my home city of Portsmouth was just what I needed to develop beyond the very non-aspirational world I left behind.

I completed my professional exams by the age of 20 and was already managing the company's six person Management Accounting team. Dissatisfied in some undefined way and impatiently ready to move on, I joined Unilever at its Wall's Ice Cream subsidiary as a Management Accountant. The role required use of the latest investment appraisal techniques and working with line management to evaluate capital projects and operational methods. For me there was no involvement with any record keeping or routine report production responsibilities.

The prospect seemed to promise all the interesting leading edge stuff of management accounting without the any of the drudge parts. However,

I was soon bored out of my mind in what I found to be a stultifying hierarchical culture dominated by a huge layer of middle management that was incredibly insular and slow moving. I was rapidly coming to the conclusions that (i) I didn't like big companies and (ii) there was more to life than being an accountant.

In contrast to my feelings about accountancy, I became fascinated by the concept of Marketing, having heard about it in the coursework for the 'Management' paper of my accounting studies and seeing marketing managers at Walls as the glamour boys (no girls in 1970) of the business. I started to study at night school for the Diploma in Marketing as an exit route from accounting.

A year into my marketing course, I first heard about Business Schools and their relatively recent arrival in the UK. With real conviction that it was right for me, I applied to do an MBA at London Business School and was accepted as one of their first two non graduates for a two year course. I owe a lot to the Old Etonian Professor of Finance, David Myddleton, who interviewed me. As I would soon discover, I was an unconventional choice at that stage of the Business School's development.

3.1.3 London Business School

There were 100 students enrolled on my course. About half of them had been to public school. Many of those and several others were Oxbridge graduates. Business Schools at this early fragile stage were very concerned to establish academic respectability and a first class Oxford degree holder was attractive to them, even when the holder had absolutely no experience outside school and university. There was also the novelty of meeting a few students and many faculty members from other countries – that was also unusual in the UK in 1970. Collectively and individually the background of my contemporaries highlighted what a confined, narrow and parochial history and outlook I brought with me.

An obvious and important discovery was that many fellow students seemed to carry a 'world is my oyster' and 'we can choose whatever we want to do' outlook. In contrast, I realised that I had previously assumed that most of the world (geographically and metaphorically) wasn't for the likes of me. The blinkers were removed from my eyes, my ambitions raised and I began to eagerly anticipate a very different future – particularly looking forward to catching up on international travel.

Over the next two years I found that I could more than keep up with most of my classmates in academic assessments with my results placing me well inside the leading group. My social life centred on a group of friends who also lived on campus on the Outer Circle of Regent's Park, London (the best address I'll ever have) and playing for the School football team in the University of London league. In every respect these were two of the best years of my life. However, I can now see that I was still operating within my comfort zone for I was very quiet in class and did not make the most of my opportunities to voice opinions and/or stand at the front and take a lead.

Different personalities are inevitable and valuable in any team

In the tradition of Harvard, the long established doyen of Business Schools, learning at the London Business School centred on the use of case studies.

Each year group was organised into syndicates of ten students who would work together across all subjects for around ten weeks before being reshuffled at the start of the following term.

For each of the several assignments per week the group would discuss the case and then prepare its answer. Typically that answer would be presented by one nominated member of the syndicate to the whole year group, or perhaps half of it, and the lecturer. The presentation would be followed by general discussion including challenges to the speaker. The team's solution could be assessed with the marks being applied to all members of the syndicate so the content and delivery of our answer mattered to us in every sense.

I froze at the prospect of making these presentations so you can imagine my initial surprise when a member of my group readily volunteered to do it. He was not alone, for in each of the six syndicates to which I belonged over a two year period there were always a couple of people with a similar enthusiasm for standing up to speak before an audience.

As we handled our first few cases other personal enthusiasms emerged. We realised that we had two dedicated technicians in the group, who were always prepared, indeed needed, to work on the detailed analysis and any statistical or mathematical aspects of the case. They would use the new facility of computer terminals to produce their models to develop and support our solution and often worked into the early hours of the morning. They were nerds.

The middle majority between these extreme types was by no means homogeneous. There were talented, hardworking and versatile individuals who could move across the spectrum at will and others who were passengers normally by inclination rather than ability.

In other words these bunches of individuals arbitrarily thrown together each represented a typical range and distribution of personality types, attitudes and behaviours. It was easy to dislike and undervalue some individuals and what they represented; and I did.

It took me a long time to realise that there is no single right way of thinking or best personal style. Furthermore, the differences are to be cherished and complementary personality types sought to make their various contributions to an effective team.

That knowledge is reasonably obvious to most of us. Remembering to actively observe the natural contribution of each individual, to value it and then utilise it requires us to remember what we know in this respect. Knowledge alone is not enough; it has to be applied.

Time went rapidly, graduation drew near and it was time to think about my next job. Consistent with all the electives that I had taken in International Business and Marketing, I applied for expatriate positions with multi-national corporations. I was quite close to choosing between opportunities in Brussels and Lagos (I may not have been optimising the international bit) when I received a phone call that changed my direction as drastically as attending Business School had uplifted my ambition.

Knowledge is No Substitute for Action

London Business School was a watershed experience for me. It significantly raised my aspirations and my confidence levels although still within the context of working my way up through an organisation as a professional manager. Having still not defined those aspirations clearly or with conviction, my next step remained subject to random influence.

That raised confidence was also restricted to the examination room and around the notion of being an MBA from a leading business school. Both have some validity but are of little use if not accompanied by a readiness to turn into action; to stick one's head above the parapet. My confidence did not yet extend to that level.

Knowledge and general intentions are not enough. Specific goals are essential and one needs enough courage to take the actions to achieve them.

A friend of mine, Geoff Hester called to tell me that he was now full time manager with a little Gloucestershire based house builder called Westbury Homes. He had been doing some part time site surveying when I had last seen him two years previously. He told me "things are going pretty well and it is time to appoint an in house Accountant". He asked if I would be interested in filling the post. I was pretty snooty. "Well Geoff" I said "I'm not an Accountant any more. I'm an International Marketing Executive". Not to be put off he told me that he had actually met a few candidates who "didn't really seem to be on the same wavelength" so invited me to come down to see him and advise on where they were "going wrong" in their approach to recruitment. The result was inevitable.

3.1.4 In Family Service

I visited Westbury Homes' offices at The Harbourmaster's House, The Docks, Gloucester, a two up - two down industrial cottage and a generally unlikely setting for a business powerhouse. That first impression was misleading. I met three people whose determination to build an exceptional business was absolutely palpable. The need and scope for a fourth player to bottle their energies and creativity and turn Westbury into a serious business proposition was too good to miss. Benefiting from, but not enticed by, a financial package beyond twice the going rate for an 'international marketing executive' I started work with them a few weeks later.

The priorities were to install processes, write business plans good enough to raise finance and bring professionalism to strategy and operations. It was great fun. Geoff, who was now Managing Director, and I were in our mid twenties and given great freedom to run a company with revenues in excess of £60 million in today's terms. The representatives of the owning family, the Chairman and his brother, seemingly ancient in their forties, were happy for us to do the work.

We were in our element, really enjoying the challenge. We implemented innovatory changes from the way that house builders had operated hitherto. Several of our breakthroughs became standard industry practice over the following decade. The proprietors become immensely rich and we were paid very well for our efforts.

> ## If you pay too little you get monkeys;
>
> ### if you pay too much you get......
>
> Westbury were ambitious in every respect and ready to pay the cost of their big ideas. In the area of executive recruitment that policy somewhat backfired.
>
> To secure what were perceived to be the best people, a head hunter and very high remuneration packages were used to attract senior executives from the largest established companies in the house building industry.
>
> We wanted them to mange our operations impeccably within our distinctive ways of working. They wanted to create new strategies and brought their own ideas of processes with them.
>
> The resultant conflict led to a series of rapid 'hirings and firings' at a

significant cost in recruitment fees and severance packages as we hurried along our chosen path.

We had made the mistake of recruiting 'generals' when we needed 'NCOs'.

We would have been much better to recruit excellent lower order managers at a much lower cost who would have been happy to play by our rules rather than boardroom directors who understandably felt that they knew better than us and wanted to change the rules.

Being a Financial Director fully engaged in business strategy and execution was a long way from being an accountant – it entailed looking at the whole business, identifying where change was needed and devising and implementing progressive solutions. So why did it last only two years for me?

Once initial changes had been effected, the emphasis appropriately switched to operating systems rather than creating them. The routine cyclical aspects of financial management soon began to irritate me. A corrosive feeling of boredom was setting in when an incident occurred to confirm the reality of working for a family company. However much freedom salaried executives may have enjoyed on a month to month basis, big decisions could still be made around the family dining table – and, at Westbury that possibility became a fact.

The Chairman's architect brother paid a visit from his home in Canada. Without prior consultation with the Board or me as Financial Director, company funds were committed for the brother to set up a house building venture in Ontario with the aim of emulating his siblings' success in the UK. The housing market was on its way down and I already needed to control operations tightly to ensure that we held onto adequate liquidity margins. The Canadian decision blew that security to pieces and I decided it was time for me to go.

For the record, the Canadian business soon hit difficulties and had to be bailed out by UK executives when the depletion of its cash put the UK parent business itself at severe risk. Yet Westbury led by Geoff Hester came through strongly over the next decade to become a leading volume house builder in the UK. It ultimately floated and only after another thirty years amongst the big players of its industry lost its independence to a £643 million acquisition by Persimmon, the market leaders, in 2006.

What was I to do? I now knew I didn't like big companies and certainly wasn't going to work for a family owned business again. What a misfit!

Awareness is the First Step

Before Westbury, I had worked in organisations where there was a general assumption that senior people were more knowledgeable and capable than their staff for they had worked their way into high office by their performance in a meritocracy. I had never met an executive who held any material equity in his/her employer.

Now I reported to Directors who owned the company and plainly did not understand very much about the business at its operational level. Neither were they active outside the boardroom. They did however set very clear expectations of business performance.

The experience gave me an identity as a company director and the fun of a role in steering the whole entity. I could never return to a functional role.

It was also my first exposure to an owner managed business. Westbury turned entrepreneurship from an academic concept into a practical reality and one that appealed to me greatly.

The Westbury experience gave me role models, not perfect ones but very relevant, and the confidence that I could run a business. My attitudes were being ripened into a readiness to go independent when events gave me a push.

3.2 Running My Own Show

3.2.1 Self Employment

Any angst was short lived. Within days a Bristol based banker who had provided funding to Westbury called me having heard of my departure. He asked if I could carry out a systems review for another of his customers who was causing concern and "didn't seem to have quite the same financial control as achieved at Westbury." I arrived at that company a few days later to start a two week systems study. The brief did not remain intact for very long.

During the first day I heard unpaid sub contactors turning nasty in reception, found that a new telephone system was being removed by its finance company and chatted with the company accountant for an hour. That evening, I called the banker from my hotel (no mobiles in those days) to tell him the extent of his customer's problems and to say that I considered business failure would become inevitable. I suggested that completing my assignment would be a waste of time. He was shocked. "We had no idea it was that bad" he said "don't say anything to the Directors and let me talk to 'London'."

Do not assume how much others know.

I was shocked by this situation. In my naivety, I had no idea that a bank could lend so much and know so little of what was really happening. The rules for Westbury had seemed so demanding and disclosure so great. Yet here was a company of similar size, manifestly less profitable even on their 'optimistic' published accounts, being lent more than twice as much money. The bankers didn't know the score and were far too late attempting to do far too little.

There are many situations when we wrongly assume how much another party knows. Those situations could range from customers or suppliers across a negotiating table or our own front line staff. It can be worth pausing to either establish what the real position is and/or reminding ourselves to keep an open mind.

(For avoidance of doubt in the specific context of dealing with banks, the lesson is to stick to the Westbury style of self discipline, not to exploit this weakness – which in any event is diminished, if not removed today.)

The next day the banker rang me back and within a further twenty four hours a delegation from the bank, the directors and I were sitting around a table to confront reality. The consequences of this situation were disastrous for the company, Directors, staff and creditors but frankly good news for me and ultimately neutral for the bank.

Despite the resistance of the directors to face facts and the indulgence of the bank in giving them time to try other alternatives, the company was forced to declare itself insolvent a few weeks later. I was appointed Receiver of the main house building subsidiary with a 'Big 8[8]' partner taking a similar role for the holding company and various non house building subsidiaries that had sprung up. Our two approaches were very different. The enthusiasm and, I would claim, initiative that I brought to the salvage exercise was not mirrored by my more established and establishment colleague who seemed exclusively interested in implementing the formal procedures correctly (quite properly of course), his fees and not taking any risks.

'In today's success lay the seeds of tomorrow's destruction."

This company was called Robert Carey Limited based in Truro, Cornwall. The location is important as physical communications with that peninsula of England were not good and transporting bulk materials like bricks around its country lanes and hilly main roads was awkward and expensive. Robert Carey created a good business out of designing and building timber frame houses. So far, so good, but being a restless entrepreneur he had to go further. He pushed on in two directions – one was erecting a large factory to build whole houses (i.e. big boxes) to be transported to site and placed directly onto foundations - a great news story but hopeless economics.

Secondly, he suffered from the "I can walk on water" syndrome to which the successful business person is susceptible. He started other companies in such diverse businesses as a garden centre, an antiques shop and

---

8 In those days there 8 large firms that dominated UK accounting – it has long since become 'the Big 4'.

a smoked mackerel processing plant! Even the still successful original timber frame house building operation could never have generated the cash flows to support that lot.

The whole haphazard approach emphasises the merits of sticking to the business that one knows. It is tempting for successful entrepreneurs to believe that they can turn their hands to anything. History tells us differently.

I was really lucky to chance upon this assignment. I built out the partially completed developments (using timber frames only of course – see the panel above) and sold off unstarted development sites and the factories. I recovered all the bank's money plus interest and my success based fee was vast compared to any day rate that I would have asked for. My financial return from this appointment enabled all the entrepreneurial activity that followed for me in the years ahead.

Boardrooms corrupt?

The Directors were, or had become, useless to the underlying operations of the business and consumed with their self interest – the first, but not the last time I was to see this situation. There were two managers outside the Boardroom who had been keeping the show on the road for very little financial reward. They became my greatest allies and were absolutely indispensable to the business recovery process.

It was notable and again not uncommon that these two managers were poorly paid. A sense of duty compelled them to give everything for the cause despite the manifest unfairness of how the rewards were shared around. Great salt of the earth colleagues but, of course, they should never become enterprise leaders.

During this period, I met a very talented computer software author, Dr. Vic Forrington, at my local squash club. Lady Luck was striking again. He told me about a Financial Modelling system he had produced and on seeing it demonstrated I immediately recognised how valuable it would have been to me at Westbury Homes. I took the idea back to my successor there and before long Vic and I combined to implement a Project Funding system for them to their immediate and significant benefit. For me, the exercise opened my eyes to the attainable opportunities in a still very early stage business computing marketplace.

I was genuinely enthused by the potential of the newly arrived mini computers of that time to help managers of small and medium scale businesses. Previously only juggernaut organisations had been able to afford mainframe computers where they would be used for high volume repetitive administrative routines and remained remote from operational line executives. My initial response to this discovery was unstructured and rather unambitious. It seemed like interesting work and an attractively self directed lifestyle so I set up shop as a Computer Consultant.

In my case this equated to "the one eyed man leading the blind" for I knew only a little about Information Technology but at that stage the typical business person was totally ignorant. That's the advantage of operating in 'frontier territory' for I knew more about computers than my prospective clients - and a lot more about what businesses needed than the average computer supplier.

"Thinking of your first computer?" my brochure screamed "Talk to us first". "Us" was me.

Miraculously I started to pick up computing assignments and soon employed technical staff to add credibility to my offering and to deliver most of the work. My receivership business had grown too around such enterprises as nursing homes whose staff had walked out, pubs with no beer, architectural engineers in love with their engineering and more house builders. Recovering the bank's position in that first Robert Carey assignment was even better news that I had initially realised as I subsequently learnt the loan had been fully written off and could therefore be written back to score a really big win on that manager's Profit and Loss account.

As a result, I received a stream of further appointments from his bank which spread to its co-lenders where the failing companies had borrowed from several sources. All the companies where I did insolvency work were already heading for extinction without urgent treatment. It was challenging and lucrative work and I believe that I did more to save businesses and jobs than most other insolvency practitioners. Overall I achieved enough to give me a feeling of satisfaction.

So things were pretty good on two fronts – a stream of highly cash generative receivership appointments and a growing IT consultancy business. What could be wrong with that? Well there was the 'nice problem' splitting my time and managing my diary across such different businesses. It was almost impossible to delegate on the insolvency side and I wanted to be close to my growing IT business as it was certainly too immature for me to be too distant from the action.

There was also a slight emotional problem on the Receivership side in that, with my original sponsor having moved on, my new appointments were very much at the 'scruffy' end of the market where typically a secured lender lost patience with an owner managed business and put me in to recover their asset financing. That's a different proposition to an appointment responsible for the whole business and to a broader swathe of creditors. Bigger businesses with more of a management challenge and a greater chance of being saved as trading and employing entities were not coming my way.

I noticed that my old 'Big 8' friend who had so ineptly handled the Carey Group assignment picked up a nice juicy appointment for a well known consumer brand company and promptly shut it down. That bugged me for I knew that I could have done a better job. I reasoned that it was time for a reality check and visited a Business School contemporary of mine who now worked at the head office of a big bank. I asked him, as a friend to give me a straight answer to the question "Would I ever break into the London centric market to obtain larger corporate insolvency appointments?" He did me an enormous favour. He said "No, they'll always go to the Big Eight". From that moment, I never took another Receivership case and put all my energies into my computing business.

Identity Shapes Ambition

Once I had tasted independence, I was never going back to working for a salary. Furthermore, I knew that I wanted to build a high growth business.

Market realities gave shape to that ambition and so, at last, I met the conditions to be an entrepreneur.

I decided to transform my computing consultancy into an author, marketer and implementer of business systems – a software house.

3.2.2 Working in My Own Business

With my senior consultants as partners, I launched Minerva Computer Systems Limited on 1st January 1980. We knew only enough to realise that we needed to specialise to succeed and selected two markets in which to play[9]. We would produce an Information Technology based solution for fund raising charities and another, to offer improved production planning and control for manufacturers.

The former was a relatively small and obscure market at the time but we had seen clear evidence of its latent potential in one of our late 1970's consultancy assignments. The latter was based on our broad perception of it being a large established market where we could greatly improve on what manufacturers were currently being offered. It also matched expertise and interest that we had in house – a dangerously naïve thought process, internally focused and based on generalities. In the terms of the 'Wrong Jungle' story told on page 39 we did not attempt to climb the tree and look outwards.

We expected charities would give us a fast start and that the production systems would become the big thing over time. So what happened? Naturally, the actual out turn of events was very different to our original plans.

Within a few years Minerva was the clear and profitable market leader in the charities marketplace and our manufacturing business was a distant second string and a subsistence business. Our timing was good in the charities sector for we caught, indeed led, the upswing of IT becoming central to their much increased revenue generating activities. Our course from start up to market leaders is a good business case study in which we unknowingly foreshadowed the path so meaningfully prescribed in 'Crossing the Chasm' the landmark technology marketing book written some ten years later[10].

We developed our first customer's system to meet exactly what they needed in a way that created the framework of a package solution that would suit other charities too. We also invested significantly in our second customer's system knowing how much our credentials would be enhanced by moving on from a single customer reference.

[9] Notwithstanding a good outcome to this particular story that is one more than is necessary or optimum.
[10] Geoffrey Moore, *Crossing the Chasm* , (Harper Collins, 1991)

We were fortunate in that this second customer was The Wildfowl Trust at Slimbridge, Gloucestershire which enjoyed a high public profile and appeal as its founder, Sir Peter Scott had presented a popular television programme and migrating ducks and geese were attractive newsworthy material. Furthermore we were able to vividly and clearly demonstrate that users of our systems could attain a rapid return on their investment through more effective fund raising.

The key moment came when our Systems Designer was discussing the requirements of the Membership Director who made a chance remark expressing his concern at the elderly and ageing profile of his Supporter base. My colleague had young children and knew of their excitement about visits to the Wildfowl Centre, so he was suprised to hear this. He reflected on this comment and proposed a brainstorming session involving ourselves and marketing people to address this challenge. The brilliant result was the concept of 'Adopt a Duck' and it went on to recruit 30,000 children individually or within schools to become Trust supporters. The scheme was based on a £4 per year (i.e. child friendly) subscription which allowed the member to select and name a migrating duck or goose. In return the Trust would send them news about sightings of their birds as they migrated between Northern Europe and North Africa (an attractive educational message), a Newsletter and free children's tickets for visits to their Centres.

Entry fees paid by parents and extra traffic through visitor shops and catering added considerably to the cash raised in the short term. As the Duck Adopters' interest stimulated family involvement, two new generations of prospective full members were becoming familiar with the Trust. Attitudes to recruitment were reinvigorated and the number and profile of supporters considerably improved over the following years. This story created fantastic reference material to send to other fund raising charities and we duly went to market early in 1982.

Minerva's marketing campaign was quite straightforward, of modest cost and highly effective. Using published charities league tables as our starting point; we used the time taken to build our reference sites to obtain good comprehensive contact details for relevant executives within the 300 or so relevant charities in the UK. We then mailed and telephoned to such good effect that over 50 individuals from 30 charities (i.e. 10%

of the market) attended a half day seminar in London. That attendance clearly demonstrated a high level of interest in the emerging potential of computers to transform their fund raising[11] reflected the efforts we had made to become truly engaged in the users' business. The response to our message on the day was highly reassuring. We were hitting the right nails on the head with our marketing message.

Customers buy benefits!

Nobody wants to buy Information Technology for its own sake. Our charities had insufficient funds to meet the demands placed up them. Subject to believing that it would do the job, they were interested in buying a solution to diminish their 'pain' by investing in the means to enhance their fund raising capacity. They only wanted to buy computer systems for what they would do for them.

A sales proposition must offer relevant benefits to the purchaser and then be substantiated by strong evidence of capability. We did this and thereby established a winning differentiator by immersing ourselves in the world of our target market and could soon talk in its language to demonstrably understand our prospects' issues and offer practical solutions.

It's no more relevant to lead with the technical attributes of a software package than it is to describe the technical specification of the van used by a distribution company to deliver postal packages.

Six attendees from that first seminar became customers and we ran quarterly events for the next seven years with every one producing at least one new name client for our evolving offering.

---

11 Previously, charities had to use off line bureaux, a process that involved sending raw data to be 'punched' into computer readable form for overnight batch processing on a mainframe computer or accounting machines with little utility beyond basic record keeping.

You don't have to be big to become market leader

Market leadership is the most valuable position to hold in your sector yielding:

- A strong sales argument with individual customers perceiving less risk than with other suppliers. Obtaining a price premium is likely to be a valid option from this position.

- Customers find Market leaders difficult to ignore. Your leadership alone is a very strong lead generation mechanism because most intending buyers will want to at least use you to obtain a benchmark – and any contact is an opportunity to start selling.

- Other businesses will come to you with Partnership proposals for you offer the strongest route into a sector that interests them.

- When you evolve your product into an adjacent sector, you carry over a high level of credibility not available to other new entrants. You need not take the risk of selling new products to a new market sector - that is one 'new' too many.

The essence of the route to market leadership is to establish a uniquely compelling solution for the needs of the group of customers within your chosen market. Market share is a term for the accumulation of individual sales transactions you effect within a definition that makes combining those customers together a meaningful term. Your sales are to individual customers and, as above, they are interested in what your product will do for them. It is not only permissible, it is essential that you select the shared characteristics of entities who you will market to, to match your capabilities so closely that you have a clear competitive advantage.

For the reasons given above you are also well advised to pursue market leadership which Moore defines as 40% of the addressable market. If you decide to take up this pursuit then you also want to define your market at a level no greater than your capacity to deliver equating to 40% of it. This level of focus together with the now more accessible unique sales proposition yields remarkable benefits which will be super-charged when you become recognised as the sector's market leader.

By 1986, we employed fifty eight people. We were in good shape and a success story with a profitable 70% of our business coming from charities augmented by extensions into membership systems. Manufacturing was very much a subsistence business that had not taken off.

But markets and technology do not stand still of course. Since Minerva had launched its products, five years previously, the IT world had moved on apace. Personal Computers had arrived and developed as meaningful business tools. In more heavyweight organisational computing, new and powerful databases and UNIX based 'open' computing had arrived and so had the first primitive versions of GUI (Graphical User Interfaces) to make Minerva's character only 'green screens' look old hat. When we had started product development in 1980, the whole business was based on choosing a hardware supplier and then using its proprietary software tools to write the programs for specific business applications to function exclusively on its computers.

Within five years the pendulum and power had begun to swing irrevocably away from the computer manufacturers to the software authors led by Microsoft and Oracle. Like most of its peers the computer manufacturer we had chosen, Data General, the 'hot box' maker of the late 1970's could not cope and was at the beginning of its decline into corporate extinction. For the time being some customers would buy a solution built on proven technology, Minerva's specialist programs and customer service but that couldn't last long and we had to change.

Picking 'Whens' not 'Ifs' - A key entrepreneurial talent?

The best entrepreneurs are excellent at mitigating risk. One key talent is spotting what <u>will</u> sell rather than what <u>could</u> or <u>should</u> sell.

An example from my history is that of the Unix operating system[12]. When I first heard about Unix, it was a free[13] piece of software that would allow applications programs to run on any hardware. This was a revelation. I knew that it was irresistibly 'the future' or at least the commercially attractive part of it.

---

12 An operating system is that layer of software that allows Applications programs such as Accounting, Order Processing or Inventory Control to connect with the computer hardware that processes the user's instructions and stores data. In Personal Computer terms, Microsoft has dominated this market for more than twenty years with its MS-DOS, Windows, XP and now Vista operating systems. Unix provided the same functionality for multi user systems.

13 The key development stage of Unix emerged from Berkeley, University of California, and became widely available for free use for academic or personal work. Enhanced commercial systems did incur a cost but at far lower prices than the proprietary systems they replaced.

That was not the conventional wisdom in the early to mid 1980's. Most of the computing industry and customers' IT Directors thought that only the computer manufacturers' proprietary operating systems could ever provide the 'industrial strength' required for big business operations. They saw Unix as fine only for academics and considered that Microsoft's MS-DOS was limited to home and maybe small business computing. How wrong they were. These operating systems came to dominate their markets ten years and break the oligopoly of the hardware manufacturers forever.

When we switched to a Unix platform for our software products there was virtually zero risk in respect of market acceptance. Its market share was still very small but the momentum of change was unstoppable. Significant work in product development and marketing remained a challenge to be done well but at least we knew that there would be a market to play for. Demand was no longer speculative.

In contrast, a switch to Unix five years earlier would have been highly risky and many early adopters fell by the wayside waiting for market acceptance although a few survivors were eventually richly rewarded. Delaying for another five years into the 1990's would have left any software company playing 'catch up' and having its proprietary products under attack from more nimble competitors with significant cost and qualitative advantages.

Although spectacular successes will emerge from businesses that move at an earlier stage, their failure rate is far higher than those who successfully discern when a change to prospective buyers' behaviour is inevitable.

We needed to develop our next generation of products. In charities, it was relatively easy; the choice was limited to choosing the best systems environment and tool kit and getting stuck into re-development. We chose Oracle, at a time when it was less obvious than it appears in retrospect, and rewrote our applications to utilise the new power and user attractiveness that had become available. In Manufacturing it was different – in truth of our software was a 'me too' product. In a market where there were many large competitors we simply did not have the resources to write a really convincing system, nor could we afford it at a time when there was a great shortage of the skills needed for the new generation of software development that was breaking out everywhere (and notably around the

City of London ahead of its 'Big Bang' liberalisation of markets).

When we looked at our Manufacturing customer base we had a disproportionate presence of 'awkward' implementations – which bigger, perhaps slicker competitors had labelled 'too difficult' – sometimes for the inescapable characteristics of a particular type of manufacturing (e.g. printing, carpets, clothing), sometimes reflecting the more personal characteristics of the customer. Yet we had highly satisfied clients and a stream of good case studies. It dawned on us that we employed a remarkable group of implementation consultants and that they were not only our strength but the very essence of our manufacturing business. This led us to the radical conclusion that we should give up our tradition as software authors and buy in a product to do justice to our strength and reputation for consultancy.

We set out to find a software package written elsewhere in the world (if the authors were British they would have to be competitors) that scored all ticks in the boxes for the technology of the forthcoming 1990's (4GL, Relational Database, Open Architecture, Unix) and was credible for international businesses. It was already clear that a business aimed solely at UK manufacturing would have a hard time. Market demand had shifted to solutions for international, even global, supply chains. Our new product would have to reflect that reality.

We found a package that was head and shoulders above the rest – and a UK distributorship was available. The product was called MFG/PRO and it came from a forty person outfit called QAD in Santa Barbara, California. It was not quite the situation we had hypothesised of an American author uninterested in overseas expansion (because they could do very nicely in their home patch) allowing us to offer incremental income without effort on their part.

Karl and Pam Lopker of QAD had written their product to support their own global ambitions and that was to become a key factor in our lives some 10 years later. For now, the idea of them establishing any real presence in Europe seemed as remote as their location some five thousand miles away.

In October 1988, we took on the product as if it were our own in operational terms. We assumed that it would have bugs that we would need to fix ourselves, and were not disappointed. We 'localised' Mfg/Pro in language and spelling terms and to meet other European requirements such as Value Added Tax.

On receipt of our first tape of demonstration software, we burnt the midnight oil to enable a demonstration to an existing Minerva customer the next day. This prospect had just been bought out of a group and was going to lose access to its existing systems within a few months. They had to make a purchase decision and it had to be quick. That knowledge was a specific incentive for us to make our decision rapidly and a boost to our confidence that we were making the right decision.

Unknown to us at the time, as we negotiated hard out of instinct and the necessity to keep down our initial financial commitment, another UK company just fifty miles away was also actively seeking the UK distributorship for Mfg/Pro. They paid much more for the privilege than we did but neither of us succeeded in securing an exclusive deal. The presence and rivalry with Dudley based Largotim was also to be a major influence on our lives for many years ahead.

Creating a differentiated proposition from a common product

We were now one of two parties offering the same product to a well defined and local market. How would customers choose between us? *Prima facie*, price would be a great differentiator and both suppliers would come under great and continual pressure to discount – a great formula for an unprofitable commodity business. Actual experience was never like that.

Despite using a common underlying product as the substantive part and base of our propositions, the two parties had very different approaches to doing business and the solutions we offered were very different. For example, from the outset our competitors strongly promoted software customisation to suit customers' particular circumstances. We promoted use of the standard product without modification[14] and, we built up different ranges of ancillary products to reflect the different market segments on which we concentrated.

14 A few years previously, a model way to run a manufacturing company had been encapsulated as 'MRP2' by Oliver Wight. Mfg/Pro was in turn accredited by Oliver Wight as being compliant with his methods and so implementing Mfg/Pro, 'out of the box' offered customers a route to upgrading their way of working. This equated to a more demanding, but far more rewarding challenge for them to accept. Our highly respected manufacturing consultants were available to guide our clients' management teams through the change process.

But the point of this story is more specific. Customer service and the market's perception of it would inevitably be crucial. Both parties would say "our customer service is great, best in the market, etc". Like 'quality', a high level of customer service is a given expectation in any developed market and everyone claims they offer it. Service was more than a 'nice to have'. Good or poor implementation services could generate enormous difference in the costs of introducing a new system and even more importantly the business benefits that flowed from it.

Saying we offered the best customer service had close to zero impact as a sales message and was not a differentiator in the market place. Yet I had a conviction that Minerva would offer the better service – and certainly wanted to know if this was not true. How could I prove it?

I decided to let customers speak on a meaningful and verifiable basis. By commissioning an independent market research firm to compare the opinions of customers representing our competitors and ourselves. The survey comprised twenty two closed questions with the opportunity for additional free format comments.

This was vital, practical and urgent stuff. It was to meet a particular need in a competitive market so the answers needed to relate directly to that context. The researchers were given a list of customers to contact. It comprised three sub groups (i) our customers (ii) Largotim customers (i.e. users of the same underlying product) and (iii) customers of other suppliers using different competitive underlying products. The list did not indicate which supplier served each customer. To ensure authenticity, staff at the market research firm did not know who had commissioned this work.

This low cost exercise gave absolutely invaluable feedback. Thankfully, we came top. It was better than 'nice to know' that we were in first place; it was a high impact competitive advantage. We immediately publicised the results and customer quotes collected along the way emphasising the independent means of data collection and challenged our rivals to counter claim if they dared. The message became an integral part of both our reputation in the market and our self perception.

The internal benefit was invaluable as it gave staff confidence and a high standard to maintain. It was also a definite aid to recruiting the best people.

As we had designed the survey questions as a serious and meaningful piece of research, the pay off went even further. For the minority of responses where we did not come top, or whenever in subsequent years there was any slippage from previous attainments we marked the topic for corrective attention.[15]. We had created a valuable diagnostic tool for management as a by product of a marketing necessity.

In effect, the survey helped us to see ourselves through our customers' eyes. It became a major contributor to Minerva's business success for years to come.

Our Customer Satisfaction Survey was more than a powerful tactic; it became a symbol of and central to our strategy and it gave us the confidence to truly love competition.

Competition is Good for You

Over the following years, I was often asked about the dubious wisdom of signing up for this type of product without exclusivity. I could honestly reply that I had soon come to see this apparent flaw as a big net benefit.

The first benefit in terms of being in deadly and direct competition with a worthy rival was that old evolutionary message – survival of the fittest. If we ever became sloppy in what we did there was a direct comparison to be made and we would soon be "dead meat". The toughness of that challenge served us very well when we were competing with third parties who were not used to such fierce comparisons being made.

Secondly, the game of the opposition was similarly raised. As we were both evangelising about the same underlying product we made a lot of effective noise in the marketplace. The UK soon became the outstanding

---

[15] Initially, our single location in South West England put us in third place on a question about geographical convenience. We improved our score over time by utilising the offices of companies we acquired as group facilities.

In the first surveys, we were also concerned that our rivals, Largotim were ahead of us in 'Ease of Use.' It turned out to be a transient disadvantage. The responses reflected Largotim's willingness to customise systems. Over time, the difficulty of applying these changes to new versions of the software reversed this comparison and our policy paid off.

Coming second on other factors such as 'Range of Ancillary Products' pushed us into corrective action.

territory in the world for the product authors. Competition quite definitely enlarged the market and enabled greater revenues for each player.

Thirdly, the excellent customer service and strong relationships that we were compelled to attain became the absolute essence of how we saw off even fiercer competition from the product authors in the years ahead which I will describe later.

When I see how other software resellers and their suppliers have performed once they have exclusivity I am very grateful that we did not achieve the effective monopoly position we would gladly have grabbed if we could. Competition is a wonderful incentive to perform and evolve.

However, I am getting ahead of myself by straying into the 1990's. Let us return to the 1980's for an important moment.

In 1987, I had stepped back from general operations management other than to oversee Sales and Marketing executed through our vertical market teams and to lead the external aspects of the product renewal search which included looking at the alternative of potential acquisitions. By the end of 1988, with product renewal decisions having been taken, it was implementation time. The charities transition was working as smoothly as could reasonably be expected. It was the Cinderella manufacturing business where the going became interesting.

It became clear that Mfg/Pro was a really hot addition to our product range. I stepped forward again into the Managing Director's seat of Minerva Industrial Systems to drive it directly towards its potential. Effort, desire and urgency alone rather than accomplished sales skills produced good early results. In late 1989, I created a 'crisis' imperative to hit enhanced financial year end figures for 31st May 1990, and was rewarded with an excellent response and the required results. Minerva Industrial Systems had become an exciting place to be.

I was convinced that the manufacturing software business could fly. The group did not add anything material to that cause and in some ways was slowing us up. The new business opportunity required us to invest in staff and marketing beyond existing policies and procedures. Taking unbudgeted proposals for spending back for Board discussion was a minor, but irritating brake on Minerva Industrial Systems' acceleration.

I had created the group and still held both a joint group leadership position and 50% of the shares, yet from my new perspective as a business unit manager I came to believe that somehow we had drifted into an conservative partnership culture in which nothing was dramatically wrong but somehow "2 and 2 added up to 3.9".

Large or equal partnerships don't work

From this experience and having seen similar situations elsewhere on several occasions, derives a key message for ambitious enterprises - "no large or equal partnerships".

I can see the temptation of a bunch of mates getting together to start up a business. It will be great fun with a good team spirit but sooner or later incisive and/or tough decision making will be necessary and that's when 'benevolent dictatorship' rather than democracy is required.

I'd make this a general rule which will come to have particular relevance around the 'exit' discussion that all teams have to face at some stage. Sooner or later it MUST end. All too often I have seen the lead entrepreneur persist with a colleague who has passed his or her 'sell by date'. If a senior player in any business is not 'cutting it' any more, for reasons of competence or motivation, it is a drag on performance of the business and an inhibitor to its progress. The nettle has to be grasped and the person 'let go'.

Having been the right job holder for the x years in the past is little or no guide to suitability for the next y years particularly if current performance is off the boil. If, as I have often seen, that is a difficult nettle for the individual entrepreneur how much more difficult is it for a partnership to be decisive and act in this regard?

In early 1990, I proposed to my partners that I bought Minerva Industrial Systems out of the group. The concept struck a chord. For my principal partner and myself it was much more attractive to own "all of a half" rather "half of a whole" because of the control element that came with the proposal. We had grown apart about what we wanted to achieve so a de-merger would allow each of us to determine our future in accordance with our own aspirations. With the price settled, I became the sole owner of Minerva Industrial Systems on 1st June 1990.

From Delivery Room to Adolescence

The new business started with eight staff and sales around £500,000 p.a. I was right about the growth potential of this fledgling business. Sales were set to increase organically to more than £10 million and its success enabled creation of a group employing five hundred staff across eight European countries.

I have talked in the first person about my Buy Out. Normally I speak about 'we' but as nobody else in Minerva Industrial Systems knew about the transaction until it was completed, I think that use of the first person is justified in this case. More importantly, I both needed and wanted to turn "I" into "we" with my key colleagues in this fledgling enterprise.

Without further ado, I gave 10% of the equity each to my Sales and Operations Directors on the basis that they were going to make Minerva happen for me. Expensive? No, it was a good investment in ensuring that they stayed with me when they were vital in the early days of independence. I also believe my general predilection towards spreading share ownership widely is philosophically correct and has been to the considerable benefit of all shareholders over the years.

The first months of trading were not promising. I had chosen an inauspicious time to start a business selling systems to UK manufacturers. 1990 -1992 was one of the sharpest recessions in that long suffering part of the British economy. We went into independent life with a very strong prospect list. Our working capital of £100,000 was enough to see us through a perceived worst case trading for six months.

Our prospects melted away over the summer as the reality of falling order books and prospects hit our potential customers. We did not see any new orders for nine months until the Body Shop signed up to use Mfg/Pro in its bottling and distribution operations, yet the contingency fund was never touched. Although far from our growth projections, we found that having to attend extra diligently to our few existing customers produced additional business from them to the extent that we were modestly profitable and the £100,000 actually grew without adding any new customer names.

This early experience was a priceless message to modify our culture and outlook. For Minerva and the IT industry as a whole too much of our attention had been drawn to 'new name sales'. A new name meant a big initial order and it was exciting to run and win a sales campaign. The less adventurous business of implementing and servicing customers brilliantly is profitable and decreases risk.

Mutual value in sustained attention to current customers

We were already good at serving existing customers. All of them were giving excellent references to prospective new customers. When our order book was low, we necessarily became slightly more flexible about what services we would provide to them. From that experience, we learnt just how much more we could deliver to our existing customers to mutual benefit.

Our additional revenue with little cost of selling was of obvious benefit to us. It was also very evident that the specific extra software facilities and/or implementation services provided gave the customer a big return on their modest additional investment too.

Sometimes it was just a re-run of initial training that allowed trainer and trainee to identify a particular software facility or to raise a current operating problem to address. Important individual topics had previously given too little weight, either because it was just too much to absorb everything in the initial training or because the client could not envisage the revised operating environment and relate to opportunities within it.

By returning to those topics when an upgraded IT platform had been achieved we found potential starting points for real business benefits arising from direct changes to working practice in the factory, warehouse or office. IT was just a catalyst and enabler for this type of improvement.

Our clients enjoyed great returns from their incremental investment and beyond the immediate extra income we built even better references and case studies to help our sales and marketing campaigns.

We were selling solutions to manufacturers suffering their worst conditions for fifty years. Our experience in the early 1990's demonstrates another important message for the entrepreneur. Simply expressed, "there are always opportunities". Real entrepreneurs will not be off put by gloomy GDP predictions, high interest rates or other similarly general and remote storm clouds.

Entrepreneurship is not about selling existing products or services to the whole economy; it is about finding something new to be sold, or a new way of selling to, an infinitesimal proportion of the whole market place for all goods and services, at least initially. Macro economic numbers always disguise the ebbing and flowing of sub sectors and a multitude of individual changes. Rapid success in an entrepreneurial venture can only be obtained through a proposition that is radically different. There is always enough buying power around to afford it; the challenge is to make using it on your proposition an undeniable first priority.

In our case, there were entrepreneurs amongst our target customers already growing manufacturing companies and enjoying their own upswings. They were very much the exceptions for most were facing the need to do something radical to compete in the new order of global competition.

In fact, these customers were visionaries who had the insight and courage to work with something new to gain a competitive advantage for their companies. They were refreshing, stimulating and demanding to work with – a healthy combination when compared to working with the more conservative majority and laggards who tend to be more concerned with fear of failure than achieving positive results. This scenario helped us to recruit and retain the best staff to form a very virtuous circle.

Our opportunity was with executive teams prepared to act rather than passively accept their fate. Their playing field had clearly changed and the standards of competitive efficiency raised to new international standards. Great! That was just what we offered – an integrated information system that allowed managers to plan and execute their business more efficiently. The independently minded visionaries in our marketplace recognised the opportunity and did something about it in the early 1990's. Their more conservative, typically bigger brethren got the point and implemented similar systems in a big way some five years later.

High Probability Marketing

Minerva's marketing soon became very effective by concentrating its limited marketing budget to maximum effect on a very small sub set of the spectrum of possible organisations that our systems <u>could</u> have helped. Our chosen targets were:

- The types of manufacturer that could benefit most and readily implement our type of solution (e.g. Automotive components, packaged consumer goods, medical devices).

- Medium sized companies, big enough to afford the investment and small enough to allow relatively straightforward buying processes and our access to decision makers.

- Buying decisions had to be made in the UK.

- 'Tier 2' i.e. smaller UK based multi nationals were a particular sweet spot given our credentials to service overseas plants and meet their intra group scheduling and reporting requirements.

Within the above definition, further companies would filter themselves out of contention if our clear marketing message about using a standard system 'out of the box' clashed with their ideas. We were very clear that we were about new technology and adoption of a particular operational philosophy.

We knew that this tightly defined sub set of the whole market could easily meet our revenue needs provided that we performed well within it. This requirement became a great discipline as it necessitated working only where we could deliver great customer benefits. The result was a series of superb case studies and high customer satisfaction. Our reputation and credentials rocketed and were instrumental in attracting the next enlarged wave of customers.

Think hard about defining your market as narrowly as possible to meet your realistic revenue aspirations in any given period. Talk about the narrow range that you will do rather than the wide scope of what your product could do.

(High Probability Marketing does not exclude opportunities outside its target range. A few enquiries from well outside your identified market segments are likely to arise. They should not be rejected automatically. Subject to any opportunity cost or damage to your strategy, any such prospect should be subject to a logical Sales Qualification process, possibly with more stringent filters than your mainstream business. If they pass that test, and you can do a good job for them, go on and take the business.)

The international dimension to the new world order is even more salient than my description so far indicates. Rather than being essentially about 'manufacturing solutions for the UK manufacturing industry,' which could only be a small, diminishing and highly competitive market, we were actually in a far more exciting business. We were catching a wave of globalisation. Emergent International Supply Chains needed the support of systems like ours. Almost all our customers had an international dimension to their business (how else could they prosper?) which we were well equipped to support. Over the next few years, we worked on projects or exported software to forty countries, typically following our UK customers to wherever they wanted to do business.

After the initial delay, new orders began to really accelerate in 1992 - 93. By 1994 Minerva was a £3 million turnover business generating good profit and even more cash[16]. With our 'visionary' customers, proving our Return on Investment case to provide crucially important evidence for the more cautious elements of the market, who would follow them at a later stage in the Technology Adoption Life Cycle,[17] the Buy Out was already a big success.

3.2.3 From working in a business to working on a business[18]

So things were going pretty well. Minerva Industrial Systems had emphatically proved itself as an independent business and our prospects were excellent as our reputation was doing us proud in a market where demand was now looking healthy. Where next? As ever, I needed to be pushing on to something new.

[16] A summarised description of how this was achieved is given on Page 85.
[17] Geoffrey Moore, Crossing the Chasm, (Harper Collins, 1991)
[18] Michael E Gerber, E Myth Mastery, (Harper Collins, 2005)

> **Play to your Strengths**
>
> There was a clear pattern in my need to move on. That probably applies to people within your team, perhaps to you?
>
> It is far better to accommodate that preference than to compel them to stick around to implement or maintain an activity.
>
> Find a way for individuals to play to their strengths.

My Sales and Operations Directors were excellent at managing Minerva within its established parameters, without micro management from me. This status gave the opportunity to release me as a resource to take a new business initiative and for personal growth for all three of us.

A key strategic risk to our business had grown a lot too – we were dependent on the products of a third party, our main supplier QAD. However much we did to add value and be close to our customers, our enterprise was built on a third party's Intellectual Property. We had to assume that eventually there would be a change in QAD's positioning that would have adverse repercussions for us – and, much later, that did come to pass. The need in 1994 was to begin to reduce that risk without missing the obvious major opportunity to grow rapidly with the QAD based formula we had developed. The fascinating challenge was how to win a large portion of the low hanging fruit so evidently available and simultaneously improve our long term robustness.

From a personal perspective I wanted an independent Minerva to continue indefinitely and be largely owned by the people who worked within it. Now in my early forties, with a young family, I wanted financial security too. I reasoned that the best way to achieve these ideals would be to float the business on a stock market. That development would allow the sale of a modest portion of my shares on flotation. Subsequently each shareholder could sell at a time of their choosing. Subject to satisfying external shareholders and public markets, we and our successors would continue to run an independent company.

With this rationale in mind, I decided to promote my colleagues to become Joint Managing Directors of Minerva and focus my time to utilise our financial strength to acquire another software company. These decisions were healthy evolutions of our personal roles and facilitated continuing growth in our existing operation. An acquisition would give us an instant increase in scale and diversity, both of which were necessary to enable a stock market float.

Cracks in the founding team

Although pleased with their promotion, it was apparent that my two co-directors were not in favour of any change in the direction of our business, preferring to enjoy the prospects of rapidly rising demand and relying on being good and effective partners of QAD. Were they on the ground in Covey's jungle? (See Chapter 2.4)

The majority view would have left us very vulnerable and missed the opportunity for a marvellous journey we were to experience for the rest of the 1990's. My decision to insist on altering course is a good example of an outward looking leadership perspective properly prevailing over an internally focused managerial view.

However, with hindsight I should also have lodged the message of dissent from my two key colleagues. Their discomfort in my insistence on pressing on to a bigger and different game was to come back to damage me, as issues left to fester normally do.

I moved ahead on the acquisition aspect of the strategy which was to build a group of operating companies specialising in different vertical markets but utilising similar technologies, selling similarly priced and sized systems (a key determinant of processes and culture in software companies) and built around the same business model.

I soon found a suitable acquisition target in a Bristol based company called Systems Team. It was in a different market to Minerva but compatible with it to the extent that a credible strategy could be formed and explained to the outside world, including the Stock Market in the not too distant future. We were embarking on a 'buy and build' programme to achieve scale and an attractive profile.

To maintain clarity of purpose and branding, each operating company would retain its own established name. A new entity, Maxima Information Group plc, was set up to be the holding company and give a collective identity.

Acquisition for Growth – A new phase

There was extra strength in the specific story that arose from the first transaction. Systems Team Limited was a secure 'tortoise,' selling systems in to the public sector where it takes ages to achieve penetration in slow growth markets but returns very sound recurring revenues once established. In contrast, Minerva was now an exciting 'hare' with rapid growth prospects being greatly enhanced by the corporate world racing to adopt the type of system that we had now been selling for some time.

I learned very important lessons from this first acquisition. They have general applicability so I will describe them in some detail.

Systems Team had produced a profit of £440k on turnover of £2.6 million in its recently completed financial year and had a strong balance sheet for its size with £700k in its P&L reserve and about £400k in cash.

We agreed on a package that gave a headline price of £2.4 million made up as follows:

- A dividend 'strip' was used to pay the outgoing chairman and VC £400k out of Systems Team's own reserves and cash. The shareholding Directors who were continuing in the business waived their right to participate in this pay out.

- Maxima paid £500k in cash on completion and provided Loan Notes to pay a further £900k in two equal instalments after 12 and 24 months.

- The final £600k of deal value was paid in Maxima shares to continuing directors, thereby compensating for the dividend strip in a manner designed to reinforce their motivation to perform for the new entity.

In essence, this is how Maxima made this acquisition without raising additional funds and leaving an adequate £500k in its own bank account. With both companies performing strongly, the Loan Note redemptions were easily met with Systems Team effectively paying well over £1million towards the £1.8million cash cost of buying itself.

A couple of supplementary features were that the exiting founder Chairman was offered a Non Executive role on the Maxima board for the two years of his deferred payment which gave him comfort through the visibility of his future receipts, a continuing business interest and identity as a company director and a useful little fee. Once his requirements had been met, the Chairman could turn his attention to obtaining the necessary agreement of his other shareholders.

Unknown to me, I became known as the 'continuity option' for we were buying Systems Team to develop it and there was an important post transaction role for the management team. This secured the executive shareholders' support, which turned out to be critical. Later I saw documentary evidence to support the vendor's story that a higher offer from a large trade buyer was turned down in our favour because of the continuity factor. We bought the company for some £450,000 or 15% less than the highest bid.

The other System Team directors and key players were immediately brought into the Maxima Executive share option scheme, which they found particularly motivating. From Maxima's viewpoint, this was a positive step towards integration. It sent a signal to all existing and new staff that Systems Team was a full member of the group.

Prerequisites for complex transactions

There is a key need to focus on decision making individuals and their needs. Like any other private, and many public company transactions, this deal was driven by personal interests. In this case the Chairman was clearly the person who had to be satisfied first. Accordingly the focus was on finding him enough money to retire on. In common with many others, his 'hot button' was hitting £1 million in guaranteed cash.[19]

But the Chairman was not a completely free agent. A Venture Capitalist

---

[19] Time may have eroded the lure of £1 million as an irresistible 'carrot'. It nevertheless illustrates that paying close attention to gauging the 'magic number' or equivalent across your negotiating table is a prerequisite of smart business doing.

who held 10% of System Team's equity could have used its particular shareholder rights to block a deal if it wished. His management team could easily deter an incoming purchaser if they collectively decided to be obstructive. Once the price had been settled and the Chairman was satisfied with his deal, we would be in a position to help him sell it to the others.

If you have two parties who want to do business strongly enough a way can be found. Considerable creativity emerged from the fertile conditions of our alignment to a common goal and sharing a great desire to do the deal.

For me these were valuable lessons to be used to good effect in the future.

From Owner Managed to Owner Directed

With Systems Team in the Group, the medium term strategy was established. Minerva would replicate its UK success with operations across Europe giving it added credibility with international customers and increase bargaining power with QAD. Systems Team would acquire more public sector specialists to give it a convincing and comprehensive set of solutions in its chosen markets.

I also believed that I could create a learning organisation in which people and ideas transferred back and forth to mutual advantage. One opportunity was based on differing cultures emanating from Minerva's recent heritage as Systems Integrators and resellers of other people's products and Systems Team's 'soup to nuts' approach of developing, selling and servicing their own software.

Like many software authors, Systems Team tended to be inherently slow-moving and prone to producing too much variation in their software.

Resellers, like Minerva were likely to develop a different culture with senior managers free from the issues of software production. They tended to be more customer and market orientated. They also had the enforced discipline of having to sell solutions based on a standard product. Whilst a more difficult sale initially, this discipline subsequently led to simpler, and therefore better, post sales implementation and support.

Systems Team had the benefit of great product margins and control of product direction.

The leadership challenge was to capture the best of both worlds by cross-fertilising ideas and people.

The next four years were spectacular. By 1998 the run rate of Maxima was over £40 million p.a. produced by almost 500 staff working across 8 European countries - quite a change from 1990 as the following table shows:

	1990	1994	1998
	MBO	Minerva – just before start of Maxima	Maxima run rate
	£million	£million	£million
Revenues	0.5	3.4	40.0
Profit	0.05	0.7	3.2
Staff	9	32	480
Business Units	Minerva UK		Minerva: UK; Denmark, Norway, Sweden, Finland; Czech republic, Slovakia Systems Team: 'Continuum of care' – Community Health, Social Services, Social Housing; Membership Systems

Minerva added operations employing 130 people and producing revenues of c£10 million outside the UK. Denmark, Norway, Sweden and Finland operating as a Nordic Region had moved from a start up with no revenues to £5 million p.a. Operations in Germany, the Czech Republic and Slovakia were established via acquisitions.

By 1998, the UK had grown to sales of £10 million and the whole Minerva sub group was a £20 million operation, or forty times greater than the £500,000 revenues at the time of my Buy Out in 1990.

In Systems Team a couple more acquisitions plus organic growth propelled sales to a similar level making the Maxima group a £40 million turnover business with, I believe, a very credible strategy. I was not alone in that belief for in November 1997 a Venture Capitalist had backed us with almost £5 million at a valuation in excess of £20 million to provide the funds to make our Czech and final Systems Team's acquisitions. This was the first occasion in 20 years of running my own businesses that I had raised external equity.

Self Funding Growth from Operations

By the time that I first raised external equity we had built a £15 million turnover business in seven years without significant capital with no outside shareholders or even bank borrowing. Growth is supposed to be expensive so how was that achieved?

Naturally, we applied good practice in credit control, which many entrepreneurs find difficult, and deferred outgoing payments where we could do so legitimately. There were two bigger factors:

(i) We held expenditure growth back to levels that cash balances plus prudent forecasts would cover. This may not be feasible in all businesses but it is a great discipline that puts the focus on generating profitable revenues with what you already have. This policy may preclude taking opportunities for further growth but as we had grown thirty fold (i.e. 60% p.a. for seven years) that was not a significant issue for us. Our limiting factor was the recruitment of best quality staff.

(ii) With clear evidence that customers wanted our IT products and services, we declined to be their bankers too. We adhered strongly to our policy of seeking significant advance and interim payments from them. I often hear business people complaining that major corporate customers are poor payers who have already squeezed the life out of suppliers with aggressive price demands. Whilst there is clearly truth in those assertions, it's also true that if you really have convinced them you have something unique that they need, the negotiations need not be one sided.

Customers are the best source of funds. If your proposition is strong and you think creatively, customer remittances can begin to arrive much earlier than is commonly supposed.

It was still my aim to float Maxima on to the Stock Exchange. As my preferred long term exit route it facilitated my wish to see an independent Maxima, principally owned by people working within it. Quoted company status theoretically allowed each executive shareholder to cash in shares at a time of their choosing rather than be compelled to act together in a trade sale. In truth, I also saw a flotation as a badge of business achievement that I wanted to wear.

Having built relevant relationships and already working to the maxim "that we organise ourselves and behave as a publicly quoted company" we appointed advisers and prepared to float in the autumn of 1996. A month or so before the envisaged 'impact day' we reviewed our position and for what now seem transitory reasons decided to postpone the event for nine to twelve months.

A combination of factors led to that decision. The AIM[20] stock market had dipped a little and was not receptive to new issues. Our first half results to November were a bit disappointing with slippage of a big order conversely setting up a very promising full year scenario for the following May and the prospects of a much higher valuation at that stage. Around these tactical issues, we delayed – never to return. In retrospect that does not look like a good decision.

Go for your central goal; don't let minor issues deflect you from the big picture and 'perfection really is the enemy of good'.

Business owners are prone to losing big life changing transactions for the sake of a few percentage points, points of principle or by attempting to find a perfect solution to too many subsidiary issues.

Do not allow minor price/tactical issues to cloud your view or failure to achieve everything you want to prevent you from doing a deal. Stay rational and evaluate the whole package in what it does for you.[21]

The pressure cauldron of a large transaction is a very good place to have an established personal confidante available to keep your decision making objective.

---

20 Alternative Investment Market, the London Stock Exchange's second tier facility for dealing in smaller companies than its main market

21 And what you won't have if you do it – and what you will/won't have if you don't do it.

When we returned to the subject with decent May 1997 results in the bag in early autumn of that year, we had an extra reason for wanting to float. For the first time we needed additional capital to execute our strategy. Two acquisitions were lined up. One of them, a very attractive purchase of a Czech based company from an ailing parent, needed to be 'cash up front or no deal' so our careful cash conserving approach to acquisitions could not work on this occasion.

A trip to Close Brothers, our City advisers, produced the opportunity to raise the necessary money relatively quickly and easily at a reasonable valuation. Our main contact at Close had recently been appointed by a South African VC to help them establish a European wide technology portfolio and we would be an ideal first investment to show that they meant business. Furthermore it would suit both parties if we were to use their money for our acquisitions, further raise our May 1998 results and boost our stock market price a few months later.

I had long since promised myself and my wife a lump sum when we floated and this capital injection was a similar situation as both an opportunity and diminution of control. The South Africans offered to buy some of my shares as my first material pay out from my many years of entrepreneurial endeavour. We went for it. The new capital in the business facilitated those acquisitions and the Maxima graph was pointing strongly upwards.

"Not everything went quite to plan"

Business conditions deteriorated sharply towards the end of 1998 and the float never happened.

Problems hit me from both external events and latent internal weaknesses rose to the surface. With some embarrassment, I will start with these internal issues for they offer some very valuable lessons especially for the leader enjoying rapid business growth and becoming recognised as successful:

- I became so busy with financiers and advisers that I failed to ensure that I was taking my operational management team with me or that they were capable of the role now being asked of them.

Stay close to your team AND be able to step outside it - A critical balance

Always find the time to talk to and listen to your team.

Consider them; what are they really saying?

Be objective about their ability to do the job that you are now expecting of them. In your mind, set a new starting point by asking yourself if they would be the ideal appointees if you were starting afresh with the future challenges you know about today. Is an unchanged team the best way to go forward?

I am not suggesting a mechanical 'hire and fire' policy as you evolve your business. I know that there will be much to consider in arriving at the best decision but at least give yourself an objective starting point.

- I was doing part of the leadership job properly by focusing on the big picture, identifying the key steps to progress to my objectives and dedicating my time to them. But looked at another way my analysis was faulty in that a series of lower level issues added up to a real drag on performance and came back to haunt me. I was in a rush to construct the edifice and did not stop to ensure the foundations were sound.

When you know something is not right, STOP and fix it before proceeding.

Actually, that is not a maxim to be applied absolutely literally. There will be some shortfalls from your standards or your plan that should be tolerated, or attention deferred, as the time and cost to fix them would be a greater cost to you.

If an issue is a clear impediment to achieving your goal the decision is easy.

If it is not so, there may still be a case for intervention as your tolerance of low level underperformance could be seen to imply acceptance and the start of the corrosive effect of a general slip in standards.

- With hindsight, there was a vicious circle causing a downward spiral. The best way to bite into that circle and stop it would have been to address the first sin. Working in positive alignment with more capable senior executives would have seen those lower level problems dealt with by my team – a vivid example of "first who, then what"[22].

There can be no greater leadership skill that ensuring you **put a totally capable team in place and in alignment with you.**

Do not take on, or tolerate people who you have to manage. Their purpose is to enable you to achieve your goals by managing one part of the mission on your behalf. When they do meet this requirement you can do what you are best at – setting the vision and direction, co-ordinating and monitoring, not managing.

Perhaps, this is <u>the</u> essence of leadership?

Big changes were occurring in the outside world too. Unlike many other software players, the Maxima board had definitely realised that growth would decelerate sharply as we approached Year 2000. Remember the Millennium Bug? What we did not anticipate was the immediacy and severity of the slow down. What was even more amazing was the impact on our bigger quoted brethren in the same market. To caricature them, they had floated on NASDAQ in the previous two years and consequently had bloated coffers, bloated sales forces, bloated egos and bloated expectations. If one had added up the budgeted sales revenues of the leading ERP players for 1999, they would have far exceeded the available market several times over in a good year. 1999 was an awful year for the whole industry apart from those contractors working on last minute Y2K fixes.

With hindsight, it was obvious that IT Directors who had been scurrying to make their systems Millennium Bug proof were going to lock down their systems as the day itself approached. Many IT suppliers were so caught up in the overheated growth of the late 1990's that they thought it was going on for ever. It was not! Demand for new systems fell away to virtually nothing. There was 'blood on the streets' as the major software corporations fought and discounted viciously for the few scraps of business that were actually available.

---

22 Jim Collins, Good to Great, (Random House, 2001)

It is imperative to 'climb to the top of the tree' and look down on what is actually happening and the terrain ahead.

The second half of the 1990's was a period of tremendous growth for the Information Technology industries. Strong underlying expansion of demand as products improved and costs came down was supercharged by the phenomena of the 1997 liberalisation of London's financial capital markets, the surge of demand to render systems 'millennium proof' and the beginnings of the dot.com bubble.

Market growth had reached unsustainable levels but it was easy for industry players to never raise their heads or to fall prey to seductive but fallacious reasons that the new technologies would change economic history.

If companies were to avoid hurtling headlong into trouble with their expensive growth plans it was imperative for their leaders to stand above the hype and hubbub of everyday life. IT business leaders had to understand what was actually driving demand and the fundamental realities of their customers' worlds. Those that did 'climb to the tree top' recognised that currently fashionable extrapolations of IT industry growth did not match those realities.

Is that statement made only with hindsight? No, it was perfectly possible to foresee the post Year 2000 collapse in demand. Prominent industry analyst, Richard Holway demonstrated that prevailing valuations of web based retail businesses needed to exceed the size of the total economy to obtain a return. He could see and illustrate this obvious impossibility clearly because he was sitting at 'tree top' level looking in on the game being frenetically played on the ground,

In the ERP sector, there had to be a slow down as the majority of medium and large scale enterprise had installed new systems in the past five years and the saturation point was in sight. Most ERP companies behaved as through explosive growth could continue for ever. All of them were destined to hit the brick wall of reality. For some it was highly uncomfortable, for the rest the collision was fatal.

Maxima coped not only with the severe market recession but with a much more direct blow too. As we had long recognised, the use of QAD's software at the heart of our solutions was a 'Sword of Damocles' that could cause us difficulties at any time. We never believed the damage would be fatal and had done much to mitigate the risk - now that assessment was to be tested.

In November 1998 the sword fell. QAD announced the purchase of their other British distributor; the Dudley based Largotim and re-badged it as QAD UK. This was clearly very bad news for us. It caused great alarm amongst the Minerva management team and staff. Already heading for a millennium shut down, in a small market like the UK the word would soon go around that the software author now had a direct presence and what could make more sense than to buy from them, the fount of all Mfg/Pro knowledge and the keenest prices?

As diplomats have learned about countries it is best to assume that **companies will ultimately act in their own perceived best interests.**

In the abstract, this is a simple and obvious statement. In everyday life it is often overlooked in the belief that personal relationships will preclude hostile acts.

We had long since predicted and somewhat provided for this type of action from QAD on the basis of common sense.

We also benefited from another form of 'climbing the tree' which was a thorough understanding of the book 'Crossing the Chasm', which we knew to be the QAD CEO's favourite read, for it prescribes software authors 'going direct' at a certain stage of market development. Put even more starkly, it's in the author's interests to let distributors open up local markets and then to recoup their slice of the margins by cutting them out when market share is established.

If I had grown a little too distant from my staff in the good times, a crisis mood necessitated getting back into direct contact with them all – and I felt better for it. I gathered them together to remind them about our strengths. I could point to our strong customer relationships, an excellent brand, the range of complementary products now included in our integrated solutions and the financial power of having the unaffected Systems Team in our group. Our sole distributorships in Scandinavia and Central Europe were also a restraint on QAD's ability to act too aggressively as they needed us to service their business in those territories.

The team was galvanised into a more resolute attitude. We moved quickly to introduce another ERP supplier as an alternative offering with the urgency of the situation triggering action. Previously a long period of excessive analysis had masked a basic reluctance to accept the need for change. Any uncertainty was now in the past, we knew what we had to face.

I kept a commitment to meet the staff and keep them up to date every couple of weeks. It is important to be visible and to communicate openly in bad times as well as good.

Remarkable results were achieved over the following year. We sold more QAD product in the UK than QAD themselves. The customers let QAD know in no uncertain terms that they did not wish to see us forced out of the market and a QAD monopoly emerge. It was very reassuring; indeed heart warming, to see that customers and the broader market knew the score. Minerva's reputation for excellent implementation and service built over a decade proved to be very tangible – existing customers stood by us and new buyers still selected us.

Up to date products and satisfied customers – the golden combination.

You may recall that our Customer Satisfaction Survey had started almost ten years earlier. Its value now became even more apparent.

Our dedication to staying in first place transmitted into what we did for customers day in, day out over the years.

That dedication translated into evolving a set of products and services that continued to meet their needs. Excellent service alone may delay but ultimately not deter customers from turning to newly available innovative alternatives should they offer obvious advantages.

We now saw that effort together with great relationships based on excellent service rewarded with recognition and loyalty to make the crucial difference when times were tough.

Late in 1999, I met with Karl Lopker, Chief Executive Officer of QAD. He smilingly acknowledged that he had hoped and expected his aggressive move into the UK to bring us to the negotiating table on our knees to allow him to buy Minerva 'for a song'. He could see now his tactic was not going to work and congratulated us on that achievement.

Phew! That was close. Ironically, it was very lucky we had not pursued my ambition to be in the public eye as a quoted company.

Recovery and Exit

The outlook for Maxima was now very uncertain. It became imperative to focus on putting cash into the bank to ensure that the company would be around to flourish in whatever world the post Year 2000 era would bring. For about a year, from early 1999, the strategy was to have no strategy other than to maximise its short term financial strength. To this end I stopped any part of the group that was losing money (even promising business units such as Finland which was following the same trajectory as its successful Scandinavian neighbours) and sold off Systems Team, the original rationale for its co-ownership having become redundant. By 31st March, 2000 when the last key transaction was achieved all debts had been paid off, there were significant positive bank balances and all remaining business units were profit making. Time for a new strategy!

As I began to contemplate the future of the group in its new circumstances I thought, for the first time in years, about my future as a distinct entity in my own right, independently of Maxima. I reached a decision that surprised me and subsequently my co-directors.

The world had fundamentally changed as demand beyond 1st January 2000 was never going to return to the level of the 1990s and any recovery was going to take some time to come through. I had missed the chance to achieve my ambition of floating Maxima on a Stock Exchange and I did not relish the prospect of 'running a tight ship' for years ahead. Consequently, I tendered my resignation from the group and set up about recruiting a successor.

> **All leaders have a 'sell by' date; move out or reinvent your leadership when you choose.**
>
> With hindsight I carried on too long in the same groove in leading Minerva and Maxima.
>
> I did not stand outside the game I was busily playing and look back on the realities nor invite anyone else to do it for me. Success was unhelpful in allowing, indeed encouraging me to carry on as I was.
>
> Without a positive programme of renewal and development any leadership will become stale and eventually ineffective. Promoting awareness of this truth and motivating you to take appropriate action is a keynote of this book.

I hit lucky in being introduced to Kelvin Harrison who was a proven performer in the software and services marketplace and much better operationally than me in concentrating on bottom line performance in flat markets. Kelvin not only took over as CEO but with personal investment and bringing the 'dowry' of another business into the group became the biggest shareholder with myself and other shareholders receiving an immediate payment and carrying forward our remaining equity stake through to an AIM flotation (at last) of Maxima in 2004.

3.3 Portfolio Years

Chairman, Investor and Business Coach

So I started the third millennium with a clean break from some twenty five years of the thrills and travails of running a business and being responsible for the Profit and Loss Account and funding the Payroll each month.

For six months I did absolutely nothing business wise. Then, I set out to build a portfolio of Non Executive Directorships, an aim that accorded with my circumstances and interests. I did not need to work for financial reasons but was still far from ready to drop out of the business world completely. I enjoyed business *per se*, finding good solutions for the challenges and opportunities that occur for every business and working with bright energetic people. For me, it was important to be able to continue viewing businesses as whole rather than working at a functional level and there was no attraction in becoming embroiled in the nitty gritty of operations. At the time, it also felt attractive to avoid the ultimate responsibility for performance and demands on one's energies and emotions that go with being a Chief Executive.

I started on a trail that many others have followed and wrote to the network of VC's, accountants, lawyers and bankers that I had built up, to let them know of my availability and requirements. I had some polite acknowledgements and enjoyed some pleasant 'coffee meetings' but there was no great rush of appointments arriving in my In Box. Similarly, I applied for several advertised positions to no avail.

Plan ahead to become a portfolio director

The half year of doing nothing was great at the time. The weight of business concerns fell away from my mind amazingly quickly. I relaxed thoroughly and enjoyed a slower pace of life than I could ever have imagined keeping me happy.

But, there is a 'but'. When I returned to the business scene, it was a far less effective starting point than it would have been six, or preferably, twelve months earlier. The people I knew best were busily getting on with whatever they did and were not just waiting for my return to offer me great opportunities.

When contacting parties that I did not already know, I was joining the masses of other people, many well qualified, who were seeking opportunities too and needing to start the introduction with "I was ..." rather than "I am ...".

I have no doubt that my extended break delayed and made more difficult the start of my portfolio career. If you wish to follow a similar course, then plan ahead and lay the foundations while you are running your business.

Recognising the need to do something differently I went along to a consultancy that helps senior executives with career advice including the promise to help secure a first Non Executive Directorship position for individuals such as me. When asked to describe my requirements more fully in terms of job content, my reply included an emphasis on positions that were "worthwhile in terms of interest and business mission and actively supporting the executive team, helping people." This response prompted the consultant to recommend me to consider Coaching as a component of my ideal portfolio.

Consequently I familiarised myself with the basic concept and framework of Coaching and decided that it was indeed an intriguing and fulfilling course for me to follow. I attended relevant courses, obtained a Coaching accreditation and 'set up shop.' My policy was to 'work with people leading independent businesses or aspiring to do so via a Management Buy In or similar" for this is the group with whom I most empathise. Some of my work was as an associate of the consultancy that had encouraged me to take up Coaching and I handled a few clients from them including retired or retiring executives who wanted to build Non Executive portfolios – ironic given my own initial difficulties.

In addition to coaching, a few consulting assignments, a couple of voluntary board appointments (at the London Business School and the Gloucester Innovation Centre) and part-time study for a history degree began to push my diary to capacity. During the course of 2002 and 2003 I also joined two Business Angel Networks and made my first investments in other people's early stage business ventures. As I approached the end of that second year, it was time for another fundamental review of where I was going.

Immersion ("down in the jungle") in the stream of individual activities that made up my working life was highly enjoyable. However, when I "stood on a tree top", looked out and projected ahead, I found positive reasons to change course. Perhaps re-energised by an extended break from the front line of business I rediscovered the ambition to be actually leading rather than just advising or supporting – and I wanted the challenge of building something, or more accurately things, to ambitious worthwhile ends with continuity over an extended period. In contrast, Coaching was very much in the background and like consulting assignments, it ended without the challenge of implementation and with limited visibility of actual results.

At the beginning of 2004, I stopped marketing for new Coaching and consulting appointments and set myself to search out opportunities, now knowing what I had learnt over the previous two years, for investing Chairmanships of promising companies. Through these Chairmanships, I reasoned that I would play a lead role in shaping businesses that I thought worthwhile, working with executives whom I enjoyed working with and, hopefully, generating a good financial return to enjoy on its own merits and as a scorecard measure of success.

At the time of writing, I have chaired three companies (and successfully sold one of them already) and a vibrant Business Angel Network[23] that has been the means for some forty early stage businesses to raise over £18 million. I have been on the advisory boards of several other enterprises and now coached some twenty business leaders. This has been a great time for me as I have been able to synthesise the experience of my long entrepreneurial career and the newer lessons developed through my coaching, consulting and investing activities.

3.4 Lessons Learnt? A Useful Cocktail?

I have been privileged in my 'portfolio' phase to date to gain insights into many businesses and business leaders through one-to-one coaching, consultancy assignments and most of all investing in and chairing entrepreneurial companies.

This exposure has given me the opportunity to reflect on my own career and all those business leaders that I have seen. I have endeavoured to think about what does and does not work and what are the most frequent mistakes. What are the keys to maximise the prospects of entrepreneurial success and minimise the prospects of failure?

After a period of wrestling with them to obtain any sort of shape, I managed to place many of them into the conventional headings of Process, Skills and Attitudes.

The content was sensible but it was not 'the answer'. The sum of what fitted into those boxes was nothing like sufficient to be "the answer". Moreover,

---

[23] Business Angel' is the term given to individuals who invest money and, normally, time and expertise into early stage businesses. A Business Angel Network brings aspiring entrepreneurs seeking funding together with prospective investors of this type.

there was stuff that seemed just as important left over, ideas that did not fit neatly under those headings.

A number of such ideas that that seem individually and collectively useful are described below. Some of them relate to the 'Foundation Blocks' set out in Chapter 2 and some of them advance us to new ground.

- **The Value of the Right Perspective for Good Decision Making**

  In 2002, Professor John Mullins of the London Business School prepared a case study about a critical phase of Maxima's history in the late 1990s. As he questioned me and we worked together on developing the case it was staggering how much my perception of the issues changed and became clearer. I could now 'see the wood' having in real life been right down there 'amongst the trees' in a world that had seemed complicated and pressurised at the time.

  In the first discussion of the case at Professor Mullins' Entrepreneurs' Summer School, students quickly focused on the issues that mattered, asked incisive questions and reached great conclusions. I thought to myself, 'if relatively inexperienced people can achieve these results with the issues brought into the right perspective by time, can I through my coaching achieve the same effect for my clients by attaining the right perspective through distance?'

  I believe the answer is an emphatic 'yes' with the common conduit between any given situation and the decision maker being the case study. Access to a concise description of the material facts of a situation is a key resource and writing a key skill. Could you write a clear case study of what your situation looks like today? Given that they knew your goals, what would a class of intelligent students advise you to do?

- **Focus on a Clear Goal for Simplifying Decision Making**

  I want to be explicit about a close sibling of the previous point because of its own distinctive importance. A vivid and SMART goal dominating one's mind has compelling virtues compared to the alternative[24]. Under the current heading I include it as a great executive productivity aid for it beneficially simplifies decision making.

[24] See also Chapter 2.3.

A Crowded Mind with the Goal on the periphery

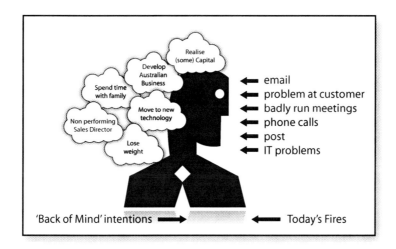

An Uncluttered Mind with the Goal dominating vision of the future

Which leader is likely to find decision making easier and more straightforward? Who will need less data to make good decisions? The pictures speak for themselves.

- **It's amazing what you can do when you have to**

I carried out some Due Diligence for a VC on a software products author. That work produced a clear 'no go' recommendation and the VC withdrew. One of the existing shareholders then asked me to help the company out of its severe cash crisis. It had used, even abused every line of credit available to it and was heading out of business on the next quarter day when several large obligations fell due.

The best phrase to describe the management team was 'paralysed, dazzled in the headlights' for despite the stark clarity of their condition they were effectively carrying on as normal. They were pinning all hopes of survival on two large orders that they expected. The latter condition is a way of life for many small software companies and the orders almost never arrive on time, if ever.

When I said they had to renegotiate with their major creditors they replied that it could not be done for they had twice rescheduled already. There were similarly negative reactions to my suggestions that they obtain advance payment from a customer who had integrated their products into large external projects of its own. They wanted to resist asking their landlord for a further rent concession and wanted to avoid reducing headcount and asking remaining staff to accept a temporary salary decrease.

I repeatedly brought them back to reviewing the hard evidence regarding the large order that they were hoping would save them. They had to acknowledge the low probability of the orders appearing in time. Then I asked them to tell me what would happen if the new orders did not materialise. Did they have any alternative remedies to prevent the terminal condition they had to project? With the facts staring them in the face they finally 'fronted up' to reality. All of my recommendations were implemented and the company saved.

Two other consequences are worthy of note. Firstly, staff morale was visibly raised despite a salary cut. The employees were not stupid and knew their company was in deep trouble. For them it was far better to suffer a little pain in the context of also hearing a clearly explained recovery strategy based on realistic assumptions that they could endorse. It was far better than what they had previously seen as the MD's blind optimism that 'something would turn up'.

As a 'lesson within a lesson' it was apparent that the MD, deep down inside, had known he was not facing up to reality and was avoiding unpleasant tasks that he knew he should tackle. Circumstances compelled him to become realistic and find the courage to initiate difficult conversations. As he came through those confrontations and was successful, he visibly grew in confidence and credibility. For him, this episode led to a permanent uplift in his performance.

Finally, the shareholders seeing their Managing Director take a grip on himself and the situation and also seeing a viable strategy came up with new money too.

Are there discussions that could dramatically change your future that you believe could never work or you cannot face up to? Think about the alternative of having held those talks and achieved what you need – then meet the challenge!

- Be realistic about the nature of dealing with large organisations

As implied above, I have seen many cases of small suppliers burning up resources over many months in pursuit of a large order from a large company or institution. Of course, some happen but far more often the prospect melts away – usually for reasons that seem unfair, illogical or just invisible to the bidder.

I recently had a good inside view of a large organisation as part of a consultancy team. We were asked to produce strategic recommendations to an organisation in the public sector, which admittedly tends to be even more conservative and slow moving that big companies. Determined to avoid just writing another large report to gather dust on the shelves, we set out to be bold and direct in our recommendations and make action irresistible.

It did not work. We did indeed get sucked into producing more and more 'evidence' and although nobody ever rejected our proposals there just wasn't any willingness to attempt actions that were very different to what was already happening. Although our direct contact had a multi million pound budget to administer he was just a 'middle manager'. He was very happy to soak up our resources in producing for data to analyse and in discussions. It was a waste of time for he had neither the authority nor the inclination to be a shape changer.

If that picture is not universal it is still representative and so I would counsel absolutely dispassionate assessment of what is actually happening in your dealings with organisations and honest realism about the amount of influence and control you hold.[25]

Realism is half the battle. The totality of your skills, processes and determination can then be concentrated on winning 'winnable' battles, a reliable path to success.

• Take Early Action to Reflect Reality

For many business people the above comments may well resonate in the context of selling to large organisations. If that is part of your life, you may consider whether to continue with low probability tactics, which necessitate whatever high level of resources is needed for the required result, or if you are resource constrained as many small companies are. Alternatively, you can change the odds in your favour.

If you were told, 'it's vital to get to the top decision maker in a sales situation' you would probably yawn and reply, 'tell me something new.' But, most of us do not actually practise this truth. In fact, there is a large sales training industry that prescribes processes to start at the bottom and work your way up the organisation. The idea is that your sales executive meets with the target buyer who has a particular responsibility. From discussion with this person, their practical problems are identified and the value of a solution is quantified. Once a credible costed solution is devised the economic or return on investment case can be demonstrated and taken up the line to those accountable for the financial performance of the business. The process is logical and may be necessary but at least the early work is low probability selling.

---

25 A frequent manifestation of entrepreneurial frustration with large companies is the slow pace at which they move. This malady can strike soon after the euphoria of winning a big order. Large corporations can sign a framework agreement including a guaranteed level of first year business but then need ten weeks to create a new component number in their system to allow call offs to commence. Often I have seen corporate approval of software purchases for projects to be rolled out across a group. The programme typically falls behind schedule. The ability of any external party to accelerate pace is extremely limited yet we often spend large amounts of time doing just that at enormous opportunity cost. Perspective and realism are the keys to effective resource allocation.

In contrast, I saw an MD take radical action to convert to a high probability approach. His business produced factory level IT solutions. Most of his prospective market was organised into geographically dispersed groups. He was particularly frustrated when one prime prospect with impeccable logic for proceeding failed to obtain the required corporate officer's authorisation to proceed. How Head Office could reject such a high return on investment without obvious or objective reasons was a mystery – but not an unprecedented one.

His disappointment prompted him to dig back into historic sales activity reports and he came up with a devastating discovery. Sales campaigns had ALWAYS been successful when they started at the top and the key corporate decision maker demonstrably 'bought' the concept and the associated proposition of a big benefit to his/her company if (NB, if) the detail and substance of the proposition stood up to examination. Conversely, when the first appointment was at plant level there was less than a 10% probability of winning an order even though the call had been well qualified in the first place.

Like many other lead generation processes, his sales force was still predominantly starting at bottom essentially because it is easier and keeps people busy thinking they are doing a worthwhile activity.

In this case, the MD acted decisively. He instructed his telemarketing people to call ONLY decision makers (and tripled their commission on resultant sales) and banned his sales force from plant level visits until they had won a senior corporate executive as their sponsor. Several members of staff were uncomfortable with this 'be effective rather than busy' diktat and resigned. The remaining staff indeed became much more effective and efficient so the MD enjoyed higher sales at lower costs – a great result for incisive analysis and bold action.

I am not sure that I would have been quite as bold as my client in this case. What I am sure about is that we all continue with low probability selling when we should have the courage to take the high probability route.

What do you know you should change but are deferring?

• Add a clear Focus on the central Goal to the Right Perspective for Spectacular Results

Following introduction to a prospective investee by a Venture Capitalist, I co-invested with them and became Chairman of a £3 million turnover software house. The MD had been running the business for some ten years and now with a young family he was keen to make some real capital for himself. In fact, he was quite specific that he wanted to collect £5 million for himself and that was quite consistent with his shareholding and a 3 year Business Plan leading up to an exit at a company value of £10 million. We invested at a valuation of £2 million. All parties and plans were in alignment.

Whilst very much buying into the business and its virtues I felt that although the company was justly proud of its staff and competence it could still gain a lot from a few well chosen partnerships around the world. This was very much against the existing beliefs and ethos of the business which had a feisty independence and pride in its staff which they considered that no outside party could match.

Rather than simply argue the case around the board table I secured the agreement of the directors to 'join me at tree top level' by undertaking a limited number of meetings with external experts and some representative potential partners. I asked them to report back on what they found and the implications for strategy.

They did this in a healthy open minded way and to their credit reached the conclusion that they should adjust their policies to include a role for carefully selected partnerships in both delivery of implementation services and in sales. One attractive form of sales partnership was seen as that of a registered ISV (Independent Software Vendor) with one or more of the large ERP software companies.[26] This would open doors to the ERP companies' customer bases, which hitherto had been slow and expensive to penetrate as 'new names'.

The ERP sector as a whole had become ex growth as the market for their core products was saturated. Many individual suppliers now

---

[26] Enterprise Resource Planning. These companies provided a wide suite of software that would support all the functions of a business, typically Sales, Operations, Financials and Inventory. Their solutions would be comprehensive but, as generalists, individual aspects of their systems could often be beaten by a, so called, 'best in class' specialist. Many had now evolved collaborative partner programmes to seek the best of both worlds.

desperately needed to differentiate with ideas for something new and exciting in short supply. For them, association with a proven winner of a product in one of the few growth niches around their core proposition should be very attractive.

So the theoretical case was made and it was very quickly and dramatically proven in practice. Within weeks of a first exploratory meeting one large potential partner proposed leapfrogging a partnership arrangement and buying the company for £10 million. The offer was accepted and so a five fold return on investment was achieved within twelve months.

The MD got his £5 million early and I would say succeeded because of his unequivocal commitment to securing that specified personal goal. In the first instance, he was alert to feedback from the market that a change in structure would take him nearer his ambition and when he spotted the particular exit opportunity he clamped on to it very hard. He also avoided the temptation to raise his sights by accepting the offer once it met his requirement and never wavered from driving the process to a transaction that met his goal.

This story also illustrates the value of an informed outsider looking in on a bunch of bright but busy executives and questioning whether the have properly understood the options open to them. Yet again, the right perspective made a change in direction obvious.

- 'Personality' Traits

The more cases of business leadership, project and campaign management that I observe the surer I am that the biggest single influence on its success vests in the personal attributes of the leader. Ideally, a mix of determination, clarity and communication of vision, simplification and speed of decision making, and appropriate people skills form a set of necessary and sufficient resources.

At this point, I should apologise to my coaching friends for my terminology. It is 'behaviour' that is the right label for the applied characteristics featured above - and 'behaviour' can be changed. I believe that change is entirely possible too. However there is some deeply engrained stuff in this set so for ourselves or someone we are already committed to working with, then let us do whatever it takes to modify our behaviour to what is needed.

However, when there is choice of who to work with, such as a recruitment situation or deciding whether to invest in an entrepreneur, I would take an absence of the required qualities as a reason not to proceed.

- A Useful Cocktail?

Perspective – Goal – Realism – Early Action – Determination – Speed – Right People

So in addition to the many specific lessons I have picked up – and the many more that you may have spotted – these few points offer me a useful over arching framework. It seems to me that all of the above factors are prerequisites for any sustained success and no amount of knowledge or functional skills can compensate if they are not present. To summarise, the struts of the framework are:

Perspective:	The world looks different from every angle and distance. The leader must select the location most conducive to producing the right strategic decision.
	Note that the adjustment to the 'correct' perspective is most often upwards, it does not have to be nor is just 'the higher the better'. '50,000 feet altitude' is not necessarily better than 'helicopter height' nor 'treetop level', for too distant a view may render vital data invisible. On other occasions, it may be very appropriate for a leader to drill down into detail.
The Goal:	Must be very clear and itself be the focus of attention from any perspective and in all decisions and actions. Equally importantly, subsidiary and side issues must be kept out of mind.

Realism: Seeing issues for what they are and understanding other people's true motivators and inhibitors as opposed to what we wish to project onto them is clearly crucial if analysis is to be soundly based.

Early Action: All the best goal setting and analysis from any perspective is wasted unless it results in action. Of course proper thought and planning should precede any material undertaking but the effective leader moves quickly to action as soon as the time is right.

It's even clearer to me that effective leaders and managers must take early corrective action as soon as recognised, whilst ineffective executives prevaricate and give situations and people 'one more chance'.

Determination
and Resilience: Nothing ever goes exactly to plan. The ability to 'restart from the wrong place' or weather severe setbacks and still hit the target are trademarks of platinum standard performers. Anyone can do it starting from the right place with entirely smooth sailing all the way!

Good people 'picking'
and Management: We have defined our ambition as requiring more than one person to expedite so colleagues will always be a vital resource. Picking the winners and handling them properly are essential ingredients of success.

Viewed as a collective set, this 'cocktail' offers a good framework for assessing the potential of a leader in pre investment situations. In ongoing business, it comprises a useful diagnostic tool when searching for the cause of underperformance. When coaching, it offers a useful guide to illustrate what an entrepreneur should work towards.

SELF LEADERSHIP AND MANAGEMENT

4.1 Almost a Philosophy

The ideas that comprised my Useful Cocktail were directly practical.

Now I want to 'chunk up' to some bigger ideas that give context to your entrepreneurial aspirations and endeavours. I am going to call these thoughts 'My Philosophy' although part of me recoils from so doing for the term threatens to take me outside my bounds of competence and be too personally revealing. This level of thinking is nevertheless fundamental in the quest to achieve true business and personal fulfilment, so must be included.

Whereas the other ingredients of success described in this book are sufficient to ensure business success, the adoption of the following, or your equivalent of it, is needed for the businessperson to be successful too.

- **Your Internal Scoreboard is the only one that matters – and it does matter.**

  Your performance against your goals or benchmarks, the way that you behave compared to your values and beliefs and how the outside world treats you all influence how you feel about yourself. It makes up the Inner You, it is your essence.

  Ultimately, nobody but you can decide how to score yourself. When other people do make assessments, you decide how to interpret it in terms of weight and meaning.

  The corollary is that your score must meet the standard that you set in every respect or you will experience negative feelings such as guilt, anger, sorrow and frustration.

  Therefore, any target that you adopt and all your behaviour needs to be aligned with this very personal scoring system that includes your moral values, sense of personal identity and personal beliefs, as well as performance targets.

• It's a Journey

Arrival points such as gold medals in athletics, promotion at work or selling a business are only interim stations. How you feel as you start, along the journey and after you achieve a major objective is just as important.

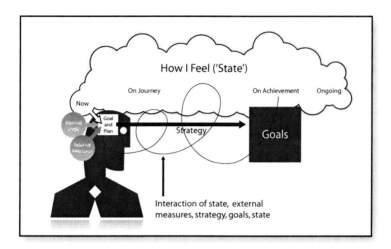

This image illustrates that our State (of mind, body and soul) is always with us. It is us. In a sense, the external Goal itself is a sub goal of the inner ambition to feel good about and in ourselves (a) as we elect to take on the goal, (b) as we work towards it and (c) as and following its achievement.

By thinking through the higher purpose of our goals we can express them in terms of our desired State, make explicit and then build into our strategy.

We need to be in the right State to do our goal setting and planning. Ideas for obtaining the required State at the outset, as we travel towards our goals and after achieving it as given in Chapter 6 & 7.

• The Whole Person must be satisfied

Undue focus on one part of life such as business success cannot satisfy the Whole Person. This is true for the vast majority of people.

Although you can feel pretty good for a long time about good performance in one aspect of your life, inattention to the others will eventually lead to feeling bad about yourself.

- It's Up to Me

  For far too long I waited to be recognised, obeying an implicit cultural message of my upbringing, 'don't push yourself forward.' I tended to mock those who declared too much ambition or whose behaviour conflicted with my ideas of normality, complained about the advancement of others and drew back from such behaviour myself. Then I realised two things:

  o that it was better to assume that nobody was going to do anything for me – at least, unless they knew what I wanted and

  o Given enough determination, all else can be obtained; I can achieve whatever I really want, provided that I actually do whatever is required to achieve it. Versatility of behaviour to act effectively is a great and essential enabler of true success. Without it, the range of objectives that can be satisfied is severely constrained.

- Values

  Matching each individual's set of values is an essential requirement for setting goals and the way they are pursued. If any aspect is ignored or contravened, sustainable success is unobtainable.

This whole philosophical area is 'Work in Progress' for me. It is Unfinished Business. I look forward to developing it more. It is central to the business of enabling people to be fully successful, in which I am engaged. I am happy to offer my thoughts as a reflecting glass for others.

4.2 Leadership Attitudes

However good the knowledge and ideas of a leader may be, he or she must activate certain personal attributes to achieve success.

Your skills and processes for handling other people are dealt with elsewhere. We now consider the internal reality inside you that foreshadows the actual behaviour that others experience from you and that governs your own ability to experience maximum fulfilment and minimum angst.

You must already have a good measure of the right attitudes to have selected this book and read this far. To the extent that any of these attitudes could be yet more conducive to releasing your full potential, the good news is that they can be developed just as much as skills and processes. Therefore, I will comment too on the rationale for modifying particular states and consider how to reach the optimal level.

You only have to compare a list including the words:

> Determined, Energetic, Straightforward, Optimistic, Genuine, Charismatic, Authoritative, Modest, Sincere, High Integrity, Confident, Open, Passionate

with one like:

> Timid, Cold, Untrustworthy, Nervous, Inert, Devious, Closed, Uncertain, Secretive, Arrogant, Manipulative, Deadbeat

to know that just the words, still more the prospect of working with what they represent makes you feel markedly different.

It is very difficult to maintain an act for very long. How one feels inside always projects itself to others over time. For the sake of ourselves, our colleagues and our combined business performance, we need to approach leadership and management with the right attitudes.

Attitudes that need to be altered can be altered. Within the bounds of business processes, goals and strategies can be modified to align with the ambitions, core values and competencies of the leader and the team. Positive attitudes will manifest themselves when this alignment is reached.

If there is a chronic misalignment and you can not or do not wish to change the external factors, it is time to look inside your head. Often a third party is invaluable, acting as a sounding board to give a different perspective as a starting point for re-evaluation. When a sticking point still exists, an NLP professional is capable of taking you right to the heart of the problem and working with you to remove the impediment. I know this to be the case.

Together with a few other Value based attitudes, Confidence is an absolute key that I will single out for some additional illustrative comments.

Confidence

Think about your own history or current activities and the difference in your approach and outcome when you do and when you do not feel confident as you take up a challenge. You will probably agree with that great managerial luminary, Jack Welch, who cites confidence as the key prerequisite to performance[27].

It is commonly supposed that Confidence is a general state of mind and a 'given' aspect of a person's character whether as a permanent aspect of an individual's character or pertaining to a particular type of situation that they may face. I believe that would be a mistaken view. Confidence can be adjusted to any required level.

Confidence is not a given fixed quotient. It is something to be managed. If it is in short supply then do something about it[28]. NLP authors, practitioners and coaches necessarily include confidence building as an intervention that they regularly deploy on behalf for their clients.

It is the same story for other attitudes that could inhibit your performance and/or how you feel about yourself. Refuse to accept any negative state as inevitable. Seek out the means to remove impediments to your complete fulfilment. It will improve your business performance and is better for you as a person.

An appropriate set of Attitudes is just as essential and just as attainable as a Philosophy, Useful Beliefs, Processes and Skills.

---

[27] Jack Welch, *Jack*, (Warner Books Inc., 2001)
[28] Sources of self development include the BBC's web site: www.bbc.co.uk/health/confidence/ and Paul McKenna, *Instant Confidence* (Bantam Press, 2006)

LEADING AND
MANAGING OTHERS

5.1 Leadership Skills

Philosophies and attitudes alone do not produce performance. Other ingredients, notably relevant skills, are also required. Business leaders have normally developed an expertise or talent especially pertinent to the particular technology or marketplace of a business – or developed from a functional role. In addition, a leadership role is likely to include the following:

Selling	Time Management
Negotiating	Team Building
Coaching	Personal Communications

Over the next few pages, I give a brief recap of what these skills are about, the benefits they bring and ideas on how to develop them. None is obscure, most are familiar in one form or another and there are plenty of good sources of further reading and training. You may already know all about what I am proposing but are you using it? And if not - why not?

Selling

In early stage businesses and other forms of entrepreneurial endeavour the ability to persuade people to change their behaviour is critical and must be achieved without the benefit of organisational power and authority. Your budget to fund supporting resources is probably very limited and your proposition often involves uncomfortable risk for others.

In short, the Effective Entrepreneur must be good at selling. It comes with the territory.

There is a wide variety of potential selling scenarios for the entrepreneur. It is very likely to include selling an investment case to secure funding. Recruitment into early stage companies or projects often requires great persuasive powers as top candidates are reluctant to take career risks and can often earn more money with big companies. And it would be rare for the entrepreneur not to be the leading sales person of the company's products or services in its early days and the following remarks are set in this context.[29]

---

29 These comments are most applicable in a business to business context entailing personal selling. Some aspects may be less directly relevant in mass consumer marketing or in e-business

Effective selling, directly to customers, is of fundamental benefit to the enterprise leader because

- With or without conventional sales skills, you are the most likely person to succeed in winning the order because you start as the most knowledgeable, passionate and determined sales representative – and to the customer, you offer the reassurance of being the ultimate authority on your business.

  Always remember that the true cost of poor selling is much more than the cost of the sales representative. Wasting an opportunity loses that prospect and the margin from the lost business, which is normally a considerable multiple of selling. That sort of loss at critical stages of a company's development can be fatal.

- Your direct engagement helpfully removes the key variable of the sales executive's interpretation of events in the field. I know from personal experience that when a sales campaign is lost it is easiest to blame the sales person (or the marketing campaign or the advert, etc) as the management team back at base naturally believe they have designed and produced a market beating solution. Conversely, the sales executive will always blame the product, price or service he/she had to offer. If you are not out there, how do you know?

With a modicum of formal sales training and understanding even the most knowledgeable and passionate entrepreneur can be more effective at sales as

- Selling is a multi skilled process where certain proven processes boost effectiveness and productivity considerably. Winning more business is the obvious reward for good sales technique.

  'Productivity' arises from the discipline of a good sales person 'qualifying out' of a sales campaign as soon as it is apparent that it cannot or is most unlikely to be ultimately successful. What is the point of any sales activity that does not produce an order? It is a classic and expensive error of inexperienced sales people to continue to pursue losing causes for too long.

- Good selling involves that old adage 'use two ears and one mouth'. The most successful sales people LISTEN and observe their prospects much more than they broadcast their product virtues and sales message. This is because they understand that selling is a matching process in which understanding of the prospect's needs and circumstances is a prerequisite of an effective sales proposal.

  The business leader who practises effective 'receiving' skills will also be good on the previous point about picking up key messages from the market directly thus enabling translation into improvements in the whole proposition. Those improvements could be the product or service itself or in its pricing or in the way that it is presented or delivered to the customer. Whatever the message, it is vital to obtain accurate feedback from the marketplace and risky to delegate it entirely to others.

The benefits of selling skills to the independent business leader are clear. How does one become a better sales person?

As with most skills, a combination of learning through iterations of training plus practical experience and noticing what works is the key. There many good sales trainers and training courses available. Take the time to learn from and with people rather than books, for selling is a social activity. Although the syllabus is not intellectually demanding, it is helpful and less costly than errors in the field to have someone else present a tried and tested map for you to utilise and adapt.

It can be difficult for analytical and technology people to accept the need for versatile behaviour and a high Emotional Quotient ('EQ') to maximise sales performance. But given an adequate underlying sales proposition it is these people skills that make the vital difference so you must overcome any unhelpful prejudices in this respect. Effective EQ is likely to become ever more important as your enterprise grows and your effectiveness becomes more dependent on working through other people. They need to be understood, led and managed too.

Negotiating

You will encounter situations where you and another party would like to do business together but where for reasons of complexity or magnitude, negotiations are required.

Useful Contextual Definition of Negotiating:

Negotiations occur when there is an approximately equal pressure/desire from both parties to do a particular deal (until then one party is still selling).

Before and during relevant discussions, it pays to stand back and consider the balance of pressure/desire between the parties.

For example, in a Business to Business ('B2B') context, considerable monies will have been incurred in product development, marketing and sales to arrive at this stage. A costly sequence is almost complete and there is a deal within sight - terms to be negotiated. Because it comes at the end of a long and expensive process it is vital that it succeeds to justify that accumulated investment. The negotiation phase determines the revenue and qualitative benefits, future costs and the type and level of risk carried. The benefits of a well negotiated agreement run much greater and deeper than merely winning the business.

In brief summary, good negotiating entails:

Recognising that only 'win- win' can work. The other party will only do what they want to do. A conclusion that is good for them enables ongoing good business together beyond this transaction.

You must be clear on your objectives too and simplify as far as possible.

Recognise that you must meet the other party's needs. For this purpose, you must know the other party's needs intimately.

Be creative about 'negotiating currencies', i.e. what are all the possible dimensions of the transaction that could matter to either side?

Evaluate negotiating currencies to establish their value and cost to each party. Asymmetries offer great scope for bringing the parties together. Something may cost you little or nothing to provide but be crucially important and therefore valuable to the other side, e.g. committing a particular project manager to a systems implementation programme or guaranteeing that after sales service will be maintained for a period to which you are already committed.

Only engage when sufficiently prepared along the above lines. When you meet, ensure that you establish appropriate Rapport with the other party before making any proposal.

Remember that there is likely to be a pattern to the discussions, which goes something like: Propose, Argue, Propose, Agree. (The mnemonic PAPA may be helpful).

Periodically, Stop. Mentally pause to 'look back in on' the scene in which you are playing to help you:

- gauge where you are in the 'PAPA' plot

- assess what you have learned about the other party and their current position

- reaffirm your objectives.

Asking for a Time Out to consider and consult is good practice.

When you have agreement, avoid ambiguity by writing it down and requiring each party to sign it and then leave the room.[30] Delivery of the bargain and shared reminiscences of how it was reached are for another day.

Coaching

I write elsewhere about the relevance and benefits for the business leader as the recipient of a professional coaching service. I also want to commend that same business leader learns something about coaching to give an additional option to his or her personal leadership capability.

---

[30] Pause to double check you are doing the right thing before YOU sign. I admit to having been sucked into a process that has taken on its own life force. What seemed right around the negotiating table did not stand up to examination when explaining it to my colleagues subsequently.

Right at the heart of coaching is specification of the right goal, setting a good plan and generating 100% commitment to achieving it, learning from the experience and developing the individual and the team to take on future and greater challenges even more effectively. What skills could be more valuable to a leader than that?

In an age when your business is likely to be knowledge-based, you employ people for their skills and hopefully their ideas, it is smart to:

- encourage full 'hearts and minds' engagement of all staff rather risking being limited by the capacity and brain power of the person at the top

- appeal to people who do not need to work for you but are bright and talented enough to find alternative employment readily if they wish.

Line executives must differ from coaches in respect of their relationship to a 'coachee'. The impact of the existence of authority and accountability for results is unavoidable. Nevertheless, adopting the approach and certain techniques of coaching still enhances leadership performance to the benefit of the individuals and the business. When you incorporate a coaching approach in your leadership repertoire you have increased your range of competent versatility – and the ability to adopt a style and techniques matched to the needs of any situation is a hallmark of an excellent leader.

Neuro Linguistic Programming ('NLP')

When I trained as a business coach there was the requirement to become certified in NLP. I had a prior perception of NLP as being rather quirky. In fact, I have found that NLP starts with a highly relevant view of the world in which I operate and proceeds to give me a range of practical skills techniques of proven value. I utilise several aspects of NLP regularly so I am delighted that I was pushed into it.

NLP originated in the 1970's through a University of California research project seeking to understand and model the behaviour of successful people. The understanding itself goes a long way to highlighting habits conducive to success and the factors that inhibit our performance. NLP has subsequently evolved to offer techniques to foster high performance behaviour and interventions to remove the inhibitors. Powerful medicine!

For the business person, NLP's usefulness derives from:

- being more alert to and understanding what individuals, including ourselves, are really saying and feeling.

- offering the means to be clearer in your communications to others – and more effective in influencing and motivating them.

- highlighting the habits of successful people to give us a comparison with our own behaviour and a first draft to develop our own model for personal use.

- awareness of the potential to remedy deficiencies, either through one's own actions or by referral to a qualified NLP professional.

The principles of NLP are in tune with long experience of my own mind and observation of others. I strongly believe that if you have a map and have a conviction about where you want to go you will get there. NLP offers such a map for human behaviour patterns and a whole series of methods to assist you on the required journey. Using only a small selection of NLP tools personally has given me a material uplift in raising my performance and that of others.

NLP is another topic for which there are endless sources of information and training and several references are given in the Bibliography.

Time Management

Planned and actual allocations of time, which may or may not be different, add up to a major influence on our effectiveness against every benchmark. It is axiomatic that good time management is a key to good performance.

Like all the skills and processes that I am citing, Time Management does not work in a vacuum. It works in conjunction with other processes and skills. For example, there is a close relationship between good goal setting and time management, which is only meaningful when geared to your well-considered and clearly articulated set of goals. Good goal setting is helped by a coaching (which may be a self coaching) approach possibly backed up by NLP techniques.

One useful and well known Time Management technique involves allocating demands on your time into a matrix whose axes are Urgency and Importance to give a framework for proactive management. The Key steps are:

(i)   List all the known tasks and desired activities on which you could spend your time.

(ii)   Allocate each item into the appropriate quadrant in the following matrix.

Covey's Time Management Quadrant

	Urgent	Not Urgent
Important	Quadrant I	Quadrant II
Not Important	Quadrant III	Quadrant IV

Quadrant II should become the focus for our attention for it will contain all those easy to defer voluntary actions that enable your big goals to be achieved.

(iii) Impose upon yourself a way of working (this is about self management) that squeezes out Quadrant III and IV items, reduces time spent on Quadrant I and therefore maximises the opportunity to take action on Quadrant II activities. Then use that opportunity and do it!

When you analyse the way you spend time you will almost certainly recognise the scope and relevance of improved Time Management to your personal effectiveness.

The drag on mental energy, from awareness that you are not tackling your big projects in addition to the loss of the key resource of time, makes a decision to review and spruce up your Time Management practices look like a very good investment.

Other Skills

I could continue with a long list of other skills that could serve The Effective Entrepreneur well. Worthy contenders include: Team Building, Active Listening, Public Speaking and Project Management.

Leadership courses themselves abound and Business Schools offer a myriad of options to suit every circumstance.

Despite the many demands on your time I firmly recommend you to allocate time to learn new skills and revisit and polish up old ones. I take this view not only because each upgraded skill can be deployed beneficially. The time away from today's operations also encourages a new perspective on them and can be a refreshing and therapeutic experience for you.

No skill or technique stands alone or gives the whole answer. You must integrate any new skill with everything else that you know. If you return from a course sounding like a textbook the effects on your credibility are likely to be negative. Adapt new skills where necessary to retain your authenticity as an individual.

Tool kit conclusion

Each of the above processes and skills has made an important contribution to my evolving performance. I am very happy to acknowledge that radical revisions of my attitudes have emanated from NLP principles and practices and directly from coaches.

For the areas that are highest priority for you, follow up this reading with further research to discover more about them. When that research confirms relevance make every effort to attend the best course or event you can find to add that skill to your portfolio. When you have covered the topics that offer the greatest direct benefit, spread your wings to more expansive subjects or just ones that really interest you. Your intuition will be a good guide to which learning options to select.

Given that you have accepted the case for change, are you 100% committed to specific timed action on your part? If not, why not? What would it take to get you to 100% commitment? Let us do whatever it takes. Action!

5.2 The Core Processes

Whatever other attributes an entrepreneur may bring to his/her business, there will be a requirement to deal with people and to cause people to do what is required in pursuit of his/her goals. People, including ourselves need clarity of purpose and to know what is expected of them if they are to be at their most helpful in this respect.

For an enterprise to extend beyond the scope of its leader's personal capacity to oversee everything that moves, a good degree of organisation and predictability is also required. That requirement is met by processes which, are essentially are applicable and transportable across all businesses. For example, there will always be the need for the business leader to lead and manage him/herself and others which can be subdivided into the processes of:

> Goal Setting, Delegation and Monitoring

> Goal Selection

> Alignment (of Self, Realities, Goals, Plans and Performance)

The following section describes a proven approach to each of these core activities.

5.2.1 Goal Setting, Delegation and Monitoring

For anyone who manages a team, goal setting, delegating and monitoring happen all the time. Is your process clear to yourself and your colleagues? Compare what you do or what you experience from your leader, with the following description of these activities as an integrated process[31].

When everyone understands a process and uses its language, there is scope for improved performance. Development of individuals and the team is likely to follow. Processes should be predictable (in flow, not necessarily in content) as the participants can then anticipate the next stage and prepare

---

[31] How the model described should be implemented will vary considerably according to circumstances. Variables that will influence implementation include relative complexity of goal and task, urgency, experience of the team and the leader, relationship between team and leader, consequences of failure, importance of goal and time frame. The description used to illustrate the process would be applicable to a significant project and is paced accordingly. For simplicity it assumes that the leader sets the Goal and outline Strategy; there will be many business situations where those steps in themselves would entail a more iterative process with the team.

for it. Conversely, knowledge of how a process works may emphasise when it is not a good idea to proceed until a prerequisite has been achieved. Simple examples of when to hold back are taking the responsibility to speak up if a briefing is not understood and not commencing action until both goal and strategy are in place.

There is no great correlation between being busy and being effective. Many people constantly work hard but never quite empty their in tray and get around to making the big changes that they dream about. Would the picture in the following diagram be one that you would recognise?

Diagram 1 – A Typical Starting Point?

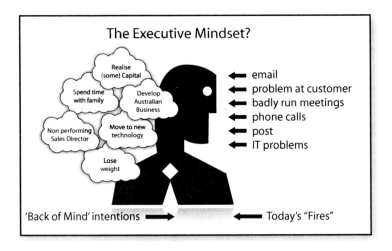

This picture typifies how issues originated by circumstances or other people come to the front of our minds pushing our big ideas to the back and away from today's agenda. The challenge is to break out of this quagmire, turn our dreams into goals and become effective in transforming those goals into actual outcomes. How can this challenge be answered? In the remainder of this book, I offer the explicit means to meet this challenge starting with the core processes of leading and managing oneself and others.

For the time being, let us assume that you have selected your project or it has been imposed and you have 'chosen' to accept. The project may be about securing a predefined outcome, a problem to solve or an aspiration to meet. Whatever the nature of the challenge you have decided that it must be undertaken and set yourself to do whatever it takes to achieve the required outcome.

Diagram 2 – A Priority emerges

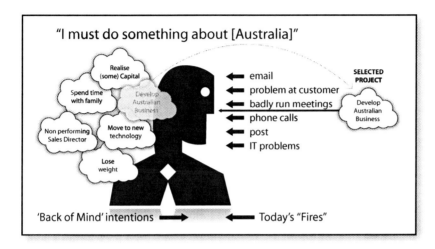

This example is based on the need to open a new business in Australia, a significant development project. The following steps will ensure that the leader is effective in realising that goal, achieves it efficiently and develops his/her team in the process.

The first requirement is to find the time and conditions to focus on the chosen project. Time has to be allocated. Other 'intentions' and 'today's fires' must not be allowed to get in the way. This second condition means not allowing interruptions through telephones, emails or people knocking on the door. Realistic time planning, a determination to adhere to your plans and a firm and clear message to others will win the time and are necessary prerequisites to start turning dreams and good intentions into reality.

Diagram 3 – Focus on Chosen Priority

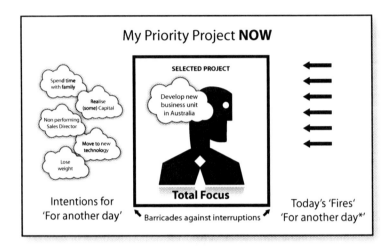

*Of course, it would be unrealistic to allow no time for everyday business and 'housekeeping', so keep some time free every day and/or every week for this purpose. Similarly, some random events or emergencies would justify over turning your planned priorities. Think in advance about the criteria you would use to decide if an interruption should be accepted or rejected.

Now go to work on the required outcome. Define it vividly for yourself. "DEVELOP A NEW BUSINESS UNIT IN AUSTRALIA" is not a SMART goal. The statement in Diagram 4 is the beginning of a SMART Goal.

Diagram 4 – Setting a SMART goal

With your clear SMART definition of the goal established a phase of self management is now beneficial. Firstly, define for yourself what benefits achieving the goal will bring to you with such questions as:

What will I get when I achieve the goal?

What will I not have when I achieve the goal?

What will I not have if I don't achieve the goal?

What will I have if I don't achieve the goal?

Still worth it? What's your level of desire to achieve the goal? If less than 100% go around the loop again – until you are 100% convinced or drop the idea.

What is your level of belief that you will achieve the goal? If less than 100%; what is in the way? Can you remove the impediments? Ask these questions recurrently during the process. The answers help to identify and remedy impediments to achieving your required outcome or could modify, or even lead to the abandonment of that goal.

When you have the 100% right answers to your verification questions it is time to think about the 'who' and 'how' of achieving your set goal.

Diagram 5 – First Thoughts on Who and How to Achieve Goal

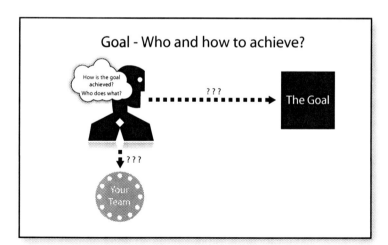

Let us assume that a high level and viable strategy can be formed in our mind.

Diagram 6 – Strategy Forms in Leader's Mind

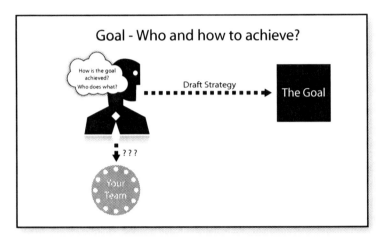

So now you know that you really want to achieve the goal, you are 100% confident that you will achieve the outcome and you have a broad idea of how to do it[32].

It is time to think about your team. Who are the people that are going to do the work to realise your goal? What do they need to do that for you? For what purpose of theirs will they do what you want?

Diagram 7 – Leader Decides What and How to Ask of Whom

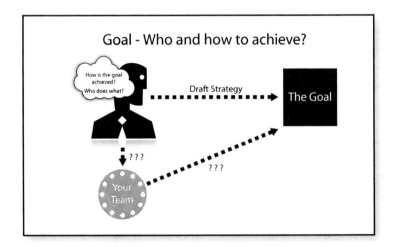

[32] The extent to which the leader predetermines strategy or takes the Goal to the team and requires them to produce it will be determined by the prevailing context.

Now think about the team, the best environment and format for briefing them – and how much discretion they will have to review and refine the Goal itself and how to achieve it. In the example, the Goal is fixed and a draft Strategy is in place subject to modification as a result of Team consultation.

Diagram 8 – Leader Engages Team

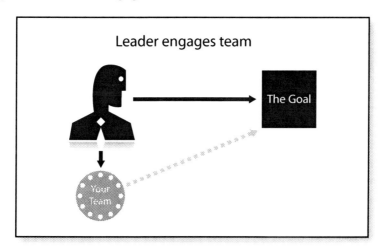

Successfully briefing the team and securing their commitment to the outcome and to achieving it is a mini project in its own right. Thought and preparation may well be necessary to successfully meet the challenge to 'secure team's complete commitment to achieve exactly what I want by the time that I leave the briefing'.

When you have assembled the team, gain their full attention and establish appropriate rapport – and do not proceed until you have met these conditions.

Explain the headline requirement; tell them why it is important in terms relevant to the team. At this stage, focus on the outcome and not how to get there.

Diagram 9 – Leader Briefs Team on Goal and Strategy

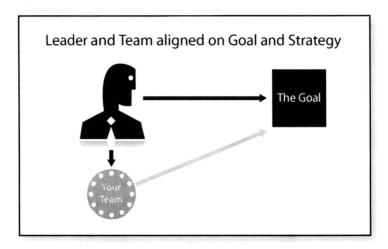

Ensure the team shares your precise idea of the outcome as you by asking them to describe it and the reasons for doing it back to you. Carefully observe the respondent for any signs, in words or body language that could indicate any doubt in his/her mind.

Diagram 10 – Validate goals, final checks (before take off)

	Leader Sign Off	Team Sign Off	Team Feedback to Leader
Clear Goal?			
100% Motivation to achieve?			
Clear Strategy?			
First Milestones Agreed?			
Adequate resources available?			
Will approach with 100% Confidence?			

There are two more potential steps to take before the leader leaves the team to get on with the job. The first, which is context specific, is to determine the very first actions to be taken in detail. Clearly deciding on and taking those first steps is the critical start of turning 'just talk and ideas' into something real and recognisable by the outside world.

Whether the leader stays to discuss (or specify) those first steps, or whether the team is left to devise them amongst themselves and then action or propose them to the leader, depends on the nature of the project, the capability of the team and the degree of risk in getting it wrong.

The second and final task, notwithstanding that all the conditions for success appear to be in place, is to hear back from the team the things that matter, i.e. the goal, their buy in, the strategy and first steps and their confident belief that they will succeed. There may be a risk of this step just being repetition but more often something emerges from this closing statement and the revelation and correction of anything that is off track now is one significant step to avoiding going off track as soon as the briefing meeting finishes. It is much less expensive to extend discussions for this purpose than to learn of any misunderstanding during implementation.

Diagram 11 – Leader and Team Aligned on Goal, Strategy and First Milestone

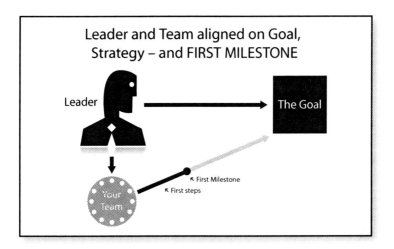

Now the game moves from ideas into action on a crystal clear basis. Delegation goes with two simple ideas that are worth spelling out because they are too often 'observed in the breach'. Firstly, the team is charged to execute the plan with leader not interfering. Otherwise, it's pretty limited delegation which both limits the organisation's management bandwidth to the extent of the opportunity cost of what else the leader could be doing and also limits development of the team and individuals within it.

In any non trivial project, it would be just as wrong for a leader to leave the team and task completely alone until the objective is reached or not. That would be abdication not delegation. Hence, the leader must monitor at appropriate intervals. What constitutes 'appropriate' will depend on a number of factors including the consequences of not achieving the goal, the risk of not achieving it particularly due to inexperience of the team and the opportunity cost of monitoring.

Diagram 12 – Monitoring progress

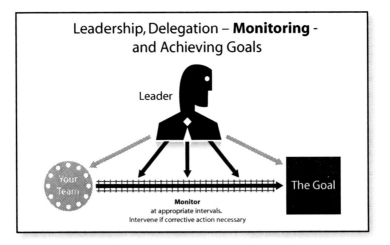

Should it become apparent that an activity is off track sufficiently to put the final outcome in doubt, then the leader should instigate corrective action. In essence that is about revalidating the goal, the 'how' and the 'whom' and then following the above process through from the revised starting point.

Diagram 13.1 – Project off Track!

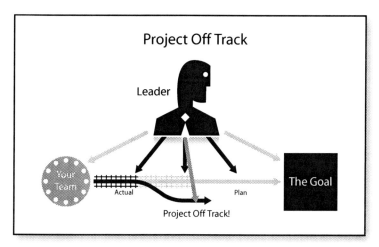

It is a true test of good leadership and management to 'start from the wrong place' and still achieve the goal.

Diagram 13.2 - Taking corrective action

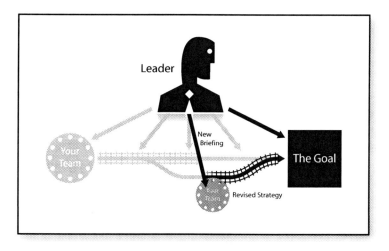

When you hit the goal remember to celebrate! If the goal was sufficiently worthwhile it should be recognised and enjoyed for its own sake and to set an expectation for future successes.

Diagram 14 - The Champagne Moment

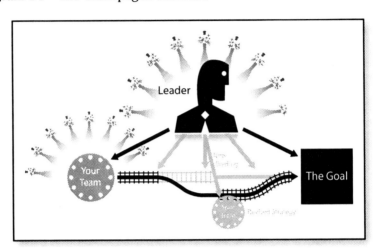

Finally, take just a short time to look back and discuss with the team what was done well, what could be done even better in the future and in conclusion remind yourself and others that you have demonstrated that you have the qualities to succeed in the challenges that you choose to take on.

Phew! We have worked our project through from beginning to end and you may be wondering how to find the time to follow this process. Do not worry on two counts.

Firstly, the process is context specific. As described, it would be a good approach to planning a military campaign but futile if a hostile gunman is pointing a gun at you. There are definitely occasions when the leader must simply issue (bark out, if need be) an order. As a more civilian illustration, the full model would be excessive to request a cup of coffee but optimal for a conference organiser embarking on a ground breaking, high visibility event that both necessitates the team's input to planning and the need to work extra and unsocial hours to execute.

Secondly, when the approach is well established and your team has an understanding of how you work, it will become fluent and move quickly. Beyond delivery of today's job, it generates a learning process from which the participants can anticipate and prepare for the next step in any future projects. It raises the team's game for future challenges so that more can be delegated and everybody's efficiency and effectiveness improved.

5.2.2 Goal Selection

The preceding process took us from defining an individual goal, good and well formed in its own right, through to its successful execution. The starting point of selecting the Goal in the first instance was, however, assumed and initial steps dealt with briefly.

A distinguishing aspect of an independent leader's life is that he/she has a great choice of available goals to select from – and it is absolutely vital that the sum of what is selected matches exactly where you want to go – and that each individual goal is a congruent component of that required outcome.

The consequences of a wrong choice of goals are likely to be severe:

- If the selected goal is in itself the means to an end, i.e. a sub goal, then clearly it must be aligned with and in support of the higher goal; otherwise, the chances of realising that end are reduced, if not eliminated.

- If the sum total of results obtainable from a set of selected goals does not add up to a completely satisfying overall outcome, it is a form of misalignment that also negates the prospects of ultimate satisfaction.

- If the goals selected do not represent optimal use of resources then top level performance is impossible. In a technology company it would be easy to 'stay in the wrong jungle,' continue to refine detail and optimise operational efficiency on current products when innovations elsewhere render the decline of today's products inevitable. Making a wrong call like that would arise from misalignment with the landscape of emerging technologies.

  Conversely, if the leader makes the right call in this respect the business can, for the next several years, 'ride the wave' of a growing market and enjoy good times even if execution is somewhat sub-optimal . If product life cycle timing is called well and execution is good then results should be spectacular – the latter cannot make up for bad judgement on the former.

- A less observable consequence of goal setting that does not make the most of available resources is to 'miss out' on opportunities that otherwise could have been taken or simply returning lower operating performance than competitors.

Goal selection can be a challenge and project in its own right, always a worthwhile one, which we may call strategic planning. In this sense, the challenge of Goal Selection begs the question of 'chunking up' to the yet higher level goals that apply to it. For business and individual, we eventually arrive in the realms of philosophy, 'what constitutes success?' and even spirituality, 'what is our core purpose?'

The starting point for great performance and self fulfilment is excellent judgement about what set of challenges you choose to pursue and the required outcome for each of them.

If the possibilities considered omit any of your aspirations then your plans must fall short of meeting the ideal overall result. Furthermore, a lingering awareness of something outside the composite goal that you have selected will reduce credibility of the path you have elected to follow and be a drag on performance.

A practical approach to Goal Selection and following through to planning and action is described in Chapter 6.

5.2.3 Alignment (including 'Good Questions' and Acting on the Answers)

Context

Before, during and after Goal Setting we are looking for complete consistency with what we are proposing to achieve, the way we intend to go about it and the way in which actual events turn out. We can call this required consistency 'alignment'.

Alignment

There are various analogies from the physical world that tell how differently both natural and man-made entities perform when fully in line or not. Examples taken from 'Connecting the Dots'[33] include:

[33] Catherine Benko and F. Warren McFarlan, *Connecting the Dots*, (Harvard Business School Press, 2003)

- Migrating geese can travel 70% farther when aligned in a 'V' formation!

- Tour de France cyclists expend significantly less energy when properly positioned to 'draught off' one another.

- A staggering 40% of Information Technology investments do not deliver what the investing business requires from them.

- More prosaically, try driving a car whose wheel tracking is out of line.

In my view the business world is often afflicted by misalignments thwarting the efforts of hard working intelligent people.

Do you recognise the following situations?

- Factories wanting to achieve low unit costs through large batches, frustrating sales people who need short lead times.

- Designers over engineering products, compared to customers' need for simple to use functionality at low cost.

- Sales representatives persistently selling the wrong products. They will favour those that are most familiar and easiest to get rather than the higher margin or newer products assumed in the business plan

and/or

Sales incentive schemes effectively rewarding strategically wrong sales.

- Customer experiences being nothing like the Chief Executive believes they are and/or should be. (How many Chief Executives phone their own call centres?)

- Financial Directors restricting resources below the level to do the required job (e.g. marketing spend constrained to an acceptable percentage of today's turnover when there is a business imperative to launch a new product or enter a new market).

- Territory and channel conflict within sales forces and between distribution networks.

- Companies perfecting yesterday's technologies when the market has moved on.

- Sales campaigns that never could have worked (e.g. very small companies trying to sell mission critical products and services directly into large risk averse organisations who will qualify them out as being too fragile – but they may succeed via established partners).

- Management's ideas of own 'slice of cake' and/or reaction to a bid approach being at odds with shareholders interests.

- Inappropriate messages being made in funding applications (e.g. when it comes to a lending decision, a banker is not essentially interested that a business can grow ten times in three years; a bank's return is based on a relatively slim margin of the amount lent so material risk is not an option. Conversely telling a Venture Capitalist that a business is sound but has no growth prospects is a quick way to the exit door).

The list of individual possibilities goes on. There's a range of potentially useful categories for all these individual cases including:

Misalignment of goals –

by intent, or simply through misunderstanding, a team can set out in pursuit of its own definition of a goal rather than the official one.

Misalignment of performance –

the goals may be aligned but the actual performance to achieve them just doesn't materialise.

Misalignment of expectations –

much customer disappointment arises from their understanding of what would be delivered and when is different to that of the supplier.

Misalignment with realities –

always dangerous and can be fatal if such fundamental external realities as market requirements or price levels are different to those understood by management.

Whatever the category, the results of such misalignments range from severe impairment of the performance through to business fatalities.

A Chief Executive Officer could also carry the label Chief Alignment Officer for nobody else has the brief or authority to bring about the complete alignment of an organisation with its internal and external environment. 'Pulling it all together' is a tough job for which the ultimate responsibility has to vest in this most senior post. High Motivation and effective Alignment go along way to creating a resilient high performance business.

I'm going to take a tour of the key alignment points of a business, initially illustrated by Diagram 1.

Diagram 1: The CEO's Alignment Universe*

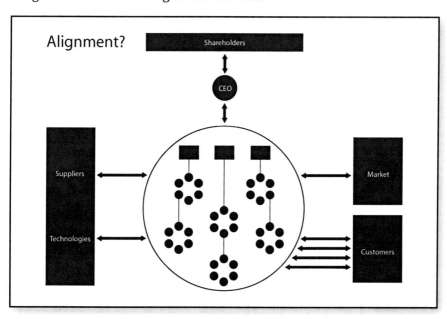

* More accurately this diagram includes only the more known and knowable layers of the CEO's universe. Additional surrounding layers such as Society, Politics and the Economy will be added later. The presence of a board of directors between the CEO and Shareholders has also been omitted for the sake of simplicity.

To start on familiar ground, we can firstly revisit the scope for one-to-one misalignment of goals with the executive team reporting to the Chief Executive:

Diagram 2: Example of Leader and Direct Report Manager Misaligned on Goal

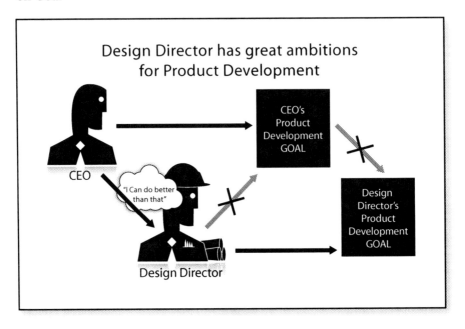

Amongst a myriad of other possible examples of potential misalignment at this level we could see Sales people (hopefully not Directors) looking for easier ways to achieve their commission than the budgeted sales mix; production seeking lower costs through longer production runs than compatible with stipulated inventory levels and Financial and line Executives wanting to contain the costs of Customer Service even when it has been rated as a strategic imperative.

When we extend our view to the challenge of aligning the entire executive team, we can see that the scope for misunderstanding the required outcome grows exponentially. Imagine the number of lines and mismatches on the following diagram needed to portray all the permutations all the alignments needed between each individual and the corporate goal and 'across the line' between individual managers.

Diagram 3: Potential for Misaligned Goals between CEO and Executive team and within Executive team

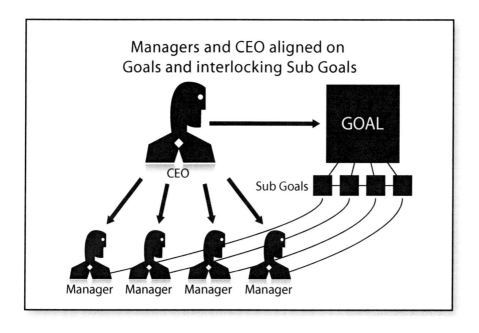

The opportunities for mismatches are (i) between each manager and his/her sub goal (ii) sub goals being inconsistent with one another and (iii) sub goals not equating to the overall Goal. The potential number of misalignments is large adding a multiplication of the number of managers and sub goals to the previous one-to-one possibilities.

With this highly motivated and capable group with whom the CEO has direct and very frequent contact, the remedies are relatively straightforward. The usual rules apply to communications to the CEO's dialogues with his/her direct team, i.e. establish rapport, be clear about Goal and carefully observe feedback at initial briefing and on a continuing basis then monitor actual performance. At this level, there is every opportunity to match remuneration packages to required outcomes as a reinforcement of good leadership.

It is more difficult and requires extra effort to ensure alignment with parties further from the boardroom. The Chief Executive must 'walk the floor' of internal operations and 'visit the coal face' of sales and customer service. It's only by actual communications with the people doing the job that the

Chief Executive knows the facts, as opposed to relying on management reports and boardroom discussion, that the message has got through to all workers and they are working to the outcome 'specified at the top' and to the strategies and performance expectation levels assumed in the board room. The CEO must talk, listen to and observe carefully everyone and anyone in the organisation. The trick is avoiding conversations being constructed as giving instructions or any criticism or other undermining of the functional heads between the CEO and the staff concerned.

Formal Management Information reports or falling customer satisfaction levels arrive after the event and therefore too late to avoid damage that has preceded their compilation.

Diagram 4: Boardroom through to 'Sharp End' Alignment

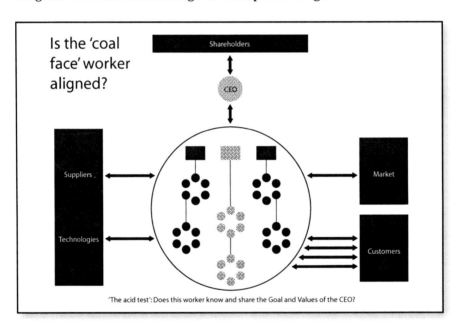

Although I am properly emphasising the 'receive' aspect of the CEO's communications there is obviously a 'broadcast' element too and it's an opportunity. The CEO can add clarity to the worker's understanding of the organisation's goal and strategy (possibly giving a new perspective for the employee who has previously received only direct micro management instructions) and boost the self esteem and commitment of the employee by stressing his/her importance in it.

This 'front line' communication boosts horizontal alignment too. Normal management processes and communications should all transmit consistently in reflection of the corporate goal and agreed strategy. A single person, the CEO, moving around departments can reduce any unintended deviations and pick up any material inconsistencies in expectation or practice.

Diagram 5: Side to Side Alignment

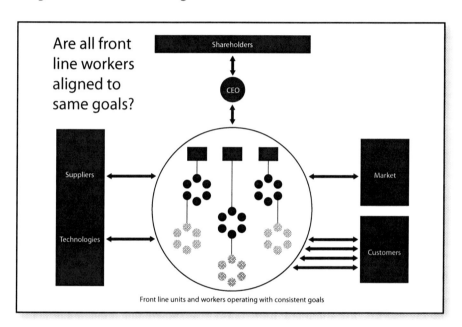

Internal alignment is important – external is critical. It has been said of quite a few business successes that they make money despite themselves. Put another way, it is impossible to succeed if a business is out of tune with its market place or other external world realities. Although no excuse for any operational complacency, an enterprise that is tune with its customers, especially if it is in a new or growth market, should be able to flourish.

On the demand side of business the crucial starting point is being in tune with the addressable market sector, i.e. potential customers whether or not they have yet bought from you. You only have a business if sufficient numbers of them change their behaviour to buy from you at the right price in the right volumes. To understand them and their needs, the more time a business leader can spend in their midst to comprehensively understand them, their behaviour, their problems, how your solution can help them, how they like to buy etc, the less likely it is that your business wastes its time and resources producing something they don't want.

Diagram 6: Alignment with Market

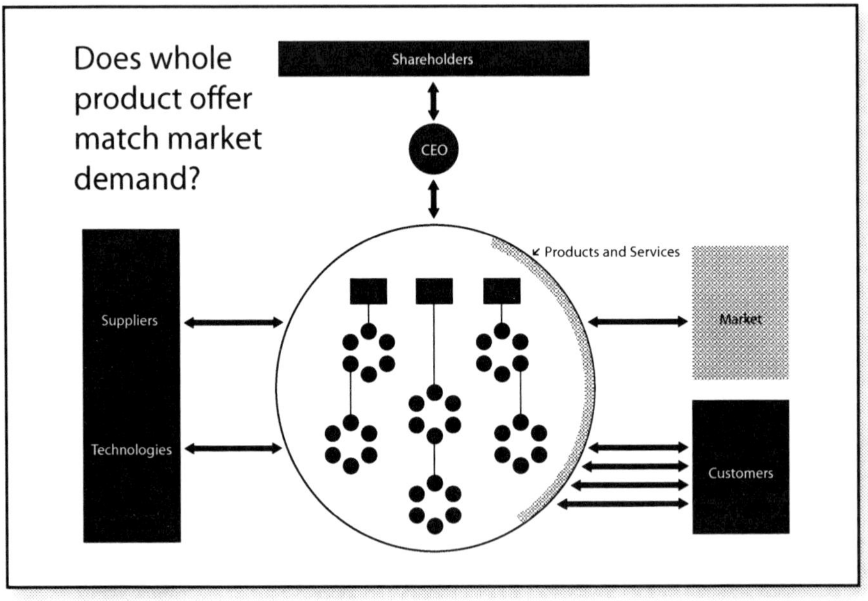

Once individuals in the marketplace have bought or decide to buy, what is their 'customer experience'? Does the response they receive, the messages they hear coincide with (a) their expectations and (b) what you and maybe your marketing team have set as the 'party line'? Is the message delivered in a way that leaves the customer feeling good - and warm towards your company.

Large investments in preparing your product and service can be quickly wasted when your front line colleagues go 'off message' or simply do not appear to value the customer.

It is worth finding a way to hear how customers feel and how members of staff have treated them. There is no simpler or better way to find that information than to ask your customers directly. If those conversations are supplemented by 'shop floor' experience to understand the realities for your staff too, then so much the better. It can be no coincidence that Tesco, the UK's business phenomenon of the past decade, insist that all managers and directors spend time every month working on the floor of their stores.

Diagram 7: Do customers receive what they expect?

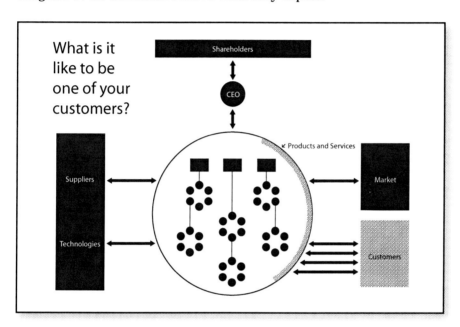

The need for similar efforts to understand suppliers and technologies is more dependent on the nature of your business and market power. If you are a reseller or a franchisee with one or a few powerful suppliers, you had better understand them thoroughly. A good personal relationship with important suppliers is obviously desirable but will not deter working in their own best interests.

Technology producers often use indirect channels such as resellers to break into and build a market share. When the market matures it would be normal to shift to a more direct to market approach. There may be good reasons that this move will not take place – but personal friendship is unlikely to be one of them. It pays to study where such a supplier may be in their perceived product life cycle.

Diagram 8:

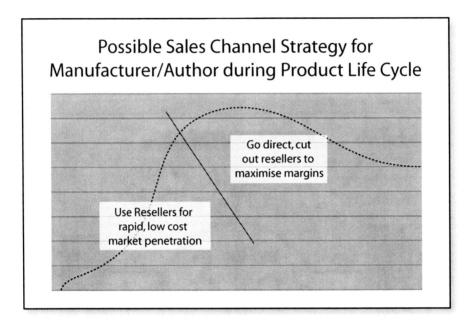

Possible Sales Channel Strategy for
Manufacturer/Author during Product Life Cycle

Go direct, cut out resellers to maximise margins

Use Resellers for rapid, low cost market penetration

Whatever the precise position of your main suppliers it is worth some time to communicate with them. Where they hold real power in their relationship with you it is clearly in your interests to ensure today's and tomorrow's alignment. In all cases, suppliers have other perspectives on your industry, technologies and markets. What else have they heard on the grapevine that could affect you?

Diagram 9: Alignment with suppliers?

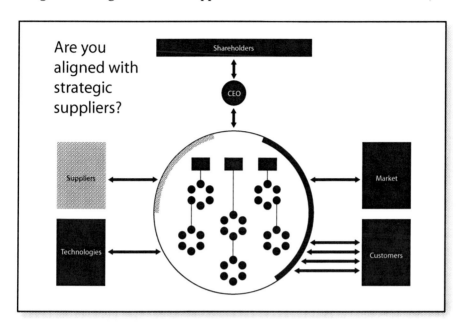

The Chief Executive must ensure that his or her company flourishes over the long term. Therefore, personal awareness of current and emerging technologies that could threaten the business is imperative. Many companies have carried on with what they are doing when the march of technology means it can only be time before the market will not want their products any more.

In the world of computer hardware, successive generations of manufacturers put an emphasis on defending the high margins of their traditional products. In every new wave of technology, the established order has been swept aside by newcomers and industry giants decimated.

Conversely, the alert entrepreneur will find new opportunities in emerging technologies. The boundaries of those technologies should be broadly defined for emergent threats can arise from seemingly unlikely beginnings. Time spent at conferences and talking to others in your industry and the creators and commentators on its technological base and reading relevant publications will inform the business leader and enable him/her to use progress to enhance their own business rather than being a threat to it.

Diagram 10: Alignment with today's and tomorrow's technologies

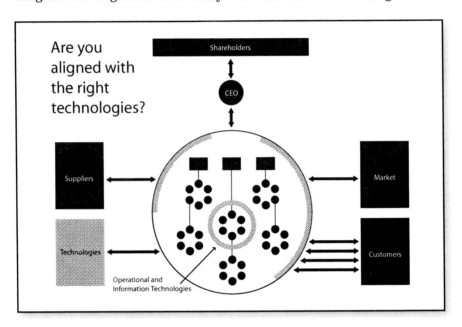

As we go around the external boundaries of the company the next group of relationships and expectations are the providers of funding, especially the shareholders who ultimately own the business.

From the providers of debt there is normally a formal and clearly understood set of expectations stated with legally binding formality. It pays to understand what those expectations are before presenting a case for borrowing from a bank. Their needs are about security and visibility. Enjoying only a fixed income, their interest is only in minimising the risk of not receiving their fixed contractual return so glitzy presentations and glowing growth predictions are not of interest.

In contrast, equity shareholders are looking for a great return on their investment. Management has a form of contract to deliver it to them. Operational performance is always likely to be very important but rarely the sole concern of shareholders.

What degree of risk will shareholders accept? How quickly and at what minimum price do they want you to sell the company? How much executive compensation will they allow for great/average/poor performance? Where shareholders and management expectations are not identical, these issues have been the cause of much disruptive angst in companies large and small. Fully understanding shareholders' expectations and matching them in aspirations and plans is essential. Keeping them informed about actual and expected results is normally high amongst their qualitative requirements[34].

Diagram 11: Shareholders and Management in Alignment?

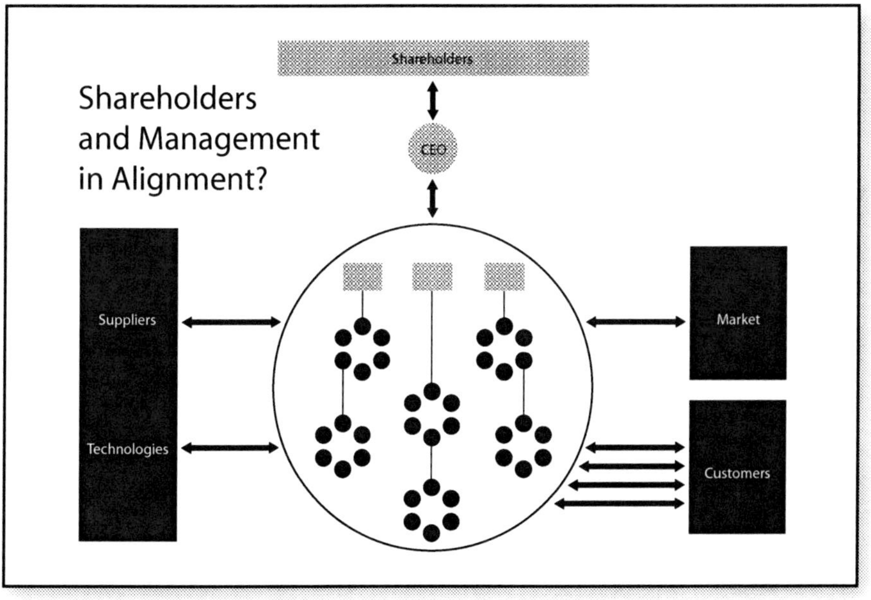

Your business and the immediate eco system of which it is a part do not operate in a vacuum. Business people should also understand and to some extent respond to changes in the economic outlook within which they operate and the societies in which they do business. Economic cycles and conditions affect things like interest rates as well as demand. Your market sector will determine how directly you need to respond to changing general economic factors.

There are always some big trends around in society. Offending current sensibilities or capturing new trends can be the difference between prosperity and failure for a business. There are a myriad of potential opportunities and potential problems heading towards us; some time should be allocated to understanding them.

34 Omitted from this description, there is another relationship in the CEO's life. It is with the Chairman whose task it is to represent shareholders between meetings. Indeed, it is a key aspect of the Chairman's role to ensure management's alignment with shareholders' wishes so both parties (i.e. the Chairman and CEO) have a formal responsibility to achieve alignment.

Diagram 12: Alignment with Universe beyond our immediate eco system

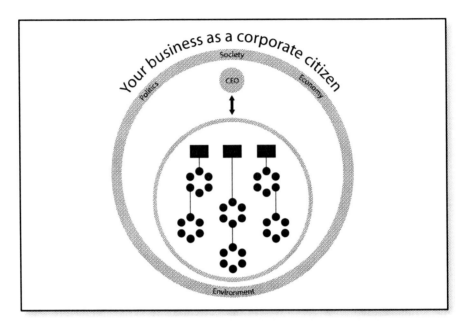

We have now completed a comprehensive tour of a business leader's universe. Feedback received during our alignment tours colours our specific map and therefore informs decisions and actions [35].

One crucial prerequisite for stimulating good feedback is the art of asking the right questions in the right way.

Good questions and acting on the answers

In the preceding descriptions of key leadership processes there has been an implicit assumption that you are receiving good information about relevant internal and external issues. This can be a dangerous assumption for there are many reasons that you may receive the wrong or incomplete information.

To steer our enterprise to a chosen point we must know where it is and the best way to get there. A good understanding of the relevant terrain is therefore essential. Information received defines the landscape of that territory, so its accuracy to an appropriate level of detail or abstraction is essential.

---

[35] It could be a good time to review your Relationship Map as shown on page 34.

Good questions appropriate to the circumstances are a vital tool of data collection.

Appropriate may be open ended with no clues to guide the speaker as to what you think or expect "What are your top 3 issues of the moment?" "What's your perception of market/technology trends?"

Appropriate may mean closed "Have you fully completed and logged all four steps of the xyz safety procedure?", "Are you 100%, repeat 100%, sure you will deliver on this date? Have you any doubts?"

Good questions are well formed, unambiguous and pertinent to the context and their purpose. I think this little story brilliantly conveys the technique and consequences of a good question.

Starting with the right question

Geoff Hester became a Regional Chairman of Barratt Homes, running a significant business with around £1 billion turnover generated from twelve geographically based sub divisions. Geoff was great at 'walking the shop' (as per a good Chief Alignment Officer – see above) in that he would always visit several development sites every week including, NB, not just office hours but weekend visits when his customers would be there.

On one occasion in the West Midlands he called into the show home. After a few minutes chatting with the sales representative he said, "Tell me about your last customer complaint."

And she told him "It was plot 32, their bathroom mixer taps leak."

"Oh dear," said Geoff. "Have there been any more like that?"

"Definitely," was the reply, "none of them like those taps – and it makes them crotchety about other things too. But it's mostly the bathroom fittings."

Note the precision of Geoff's original question – it was closed to the extent that there had to be an answer but open as to when, scope and severity. It was a great contrast to the limp "How's it all going then?" or lazy and somewhat disrespectful "Are the punters happy?"

Questions need precision in the grammatical sense and, of course, the relationship with the recipient must be conducive to receiving a meaningful answer – senior executives questioning juniors have to be especially careful in this regard. The best questions, and no more and no less, are most likely to be asked when the questioner has (a) clear fix on the required outcome (for Geoff Hester customer satisfaction was the key operational goal) and (b) the right perspective.

Most often the right perspective for business leaders means rising to the proverbial '30,000 feet above ground' and looking back in on their business and how it is interacting with its environment and what changes in the environment are coming over the horizon to disturb the *status quo*. Sometimes the perspective will change, like Geoff's, to that of 'the coal face' where the discussion may be quite detailed as it represents a sampling exercise of what is happening many times and if defective will ultimately register on a larger scale in formal business measures. The leader should also be looking to see that the 'big messages' from the boardroom are being translated into front line operations. There is a 'broadcast' element in any communication, including questions. A CEO showing a real interest in a front line colleague's work by asking pertinent questions is pretty good for morale too.

Occasionally there will be important questions that you are not competent to ask personally. If a subject is too technical, too complex, in unfamiliar territory such as a new country or simply a question that you cannot get around to because of other priorities, you may instruct others such as consultants to ask for and provisionally interpret for you. Naturally, you retain the responsibility to brief your agents to ask the right questions and to ensure that you understand enough about the answers to interpret them properly.

OK; we have asked the right questions. What happens next?

Follow Up – and how NOT to collect good information

So Geoff went on to hear about various problems at the site and certainly that the bathroom fittings were giving his company a bad name. He thanked the sales representative and returned to his car. He drove a short distance, stopped around the first corner and called the area office. He opened the conversation with his Area Managing Director by saying "Hey, Alan I've just been to the xyz site and we've a real plumbing problem there."

"Oh" came the reply "I was there last week and they didn't tell me. They said everything was all right".

In fact, in a rather hurried way (he didn't take the time to build any rapport) he had asked, "How are things, all right?" when he saw the building manager. He did not even call into the show house which was not only lost the opportunity for important information but showed scant regard for a key member of staff. A pretty useless question got the almost meaningless, "Fine, thanks" answer it deserved.

USE THE ANSWERS! TAKE ACTION IF ANYTHING IS NOT RIGHT. When successful leaders from Jack Welch downwards are asked to name their biggest regret the most frequently cited issue is that they "waited too long, were not radical enough" or similar. For example, doing something about a long term colleague who is no longer performing is easy to defer. It is tempting to give the person 'one more chance'. As a generalisation, it never works. More likely, the problem gets worse and the right course is more difficult to recover as time goes by.

Early Committed Action to Remedy Underperformance

Geoff took action "I want all of the directors here, on the doorsteps on Saturday morning. I want you to apologise to the householders for the bathroom taps which we will replace with something much better ……. and I want you to collect any other outstanding snags or matters of dissatisfaction they want to talk about. Report to me with the full picture on Monday morning."

The MD said "We could get that tomorrow (Friday) Geoff from the building manager". "I want YOU to do it at the WEEKEND," said Geoff.

The MD spluttered, "But Geoff, the FD's going to the football match, he's got the tickets and the Sales Director's going to a wedding." "I want YOU to do it at the weekend – and you're coming to see me on Monday morning anyway" said Geoff.

Geoff was taking action.

(If you think he was a little harsh on his MD, I should add that Geoff suspected this particular area management team of going a bit sloppy after a long period of good market conditions allowing them to turn in good figures and earn good bonuses. That wasn't enough for Geoff, who knew not only that they could do better but that customer satisfaction was of paramount importance not just now but in the bad times that would undoubtedly arrive when the market down turn arrived, as it inevitably would.)

There is nothing intellectually difficult about asking good questions and doing something about any misalignment that you reveal. It just requires a little thought, from the right goal orientated perspective to formulate the right enquiry and a commitment to taking the earliest possible remedial action when you identify the need.

IDEAS INTO ACTION

6.1 Your Personal Business Plan

Any author would like to hear that his/her readers have enjoyed reading their output and, even better if it has been interesting, relevant and stimulating. However for a book, such as *The Effective Entrepreneur*, intended to be practical, such feedback would be only be a consolation medal. **The real prize is action.** Without action, frustration, annoyance and under utilisation of potential will continue to be a feature of the reader's life. To have read this book with no intention of making a change would be just intellectual tourism, so what about it?

To gain a return on your time and investment you must make a change and start NOW.

When you do put into action what you have learned, you WILL create that Return on Investment that you set out to achieve.

You can start to enable it with your personalised version of the recommended process that follows.

A framework for action

Here is the process that I follow. It works for me because I know it takes me where I want to go. As a pre-condition and as a result, I commit fully to it, i.e. it is a virtuous circle.

The confidence test applies to you too, so take each stage seriously and do not complete any interim step, still less your final conclusions, until you can say 'yes' to both questions: "Do I have 100% motivation to achieve this goal? Am I 100% confident that I will achieve it?". It is good to go through several iterations of the process to arrive at this level of certainty.

1. Write down the big personal and business themes of your life: e.g. Money, Recreation, Family, Spiritual/Intellectual/Social/ Community, Your State of Mind.

2. Against each heading write down whatever the ideal outcome or state would be. At this stage don't worry whether or not it is SMART.

    - Include 'Personal Development' as a theme and be prepared

to allocate time to explicitly required outcomes or just to explore.

- Reflect your real wishes about achieving a certain 'state' or combination of states. Examples could include contentment, happiness, freedom from phobias, satisfaction. There is much truth in the old saying that 'you don't get what you don't measure' so plan and be prepared to measure everything you want.

- Invest in your Market Value. Beyond performance in your current role what else could produce valuable new opportunities for you and/or increase your perceived economic worth?

For example, raising your profile and extending your personal network through participation in your industry and/or sector's affairs is an activity that can pay off in big and unpredictable ways. It could make you a known and endorsed figure to head hunters and to companies and Venture Capitalists offering entrepreneurial opportunities. If they don't know you, they cannot offer you anything; they will go somewhere else.

Ideal Outcome - First pass

Theme		Ideal Outcome
Money	Capital	£1 million Pension Fund, Mortgage paid off, £500k in the bank, Holiday home, 1956 Jaguar MK
	Income	£150k p.a. without current stress level
Health and Fitness	Weight	80-85 kgs
	Fitness	Visit Gym 3 times a week
Family	Spouse	Getting on well, shared activity, 3 holidays p.a.
	Children	Happy and successful doing 'A' levels and at University respectively
Etc.		
Etc.		

3. Now choose an actual date (e.g. Thursday, 17th July 2010 - not 'in 3 years time') where you can reasonably clearly define what you want from the most central/addressable theme. I use a possible core business objective to illustrate in the following steps.

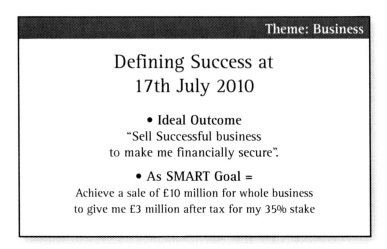

4. Now for each of your themes become specific and define what you will achieve for each of them at this same date.

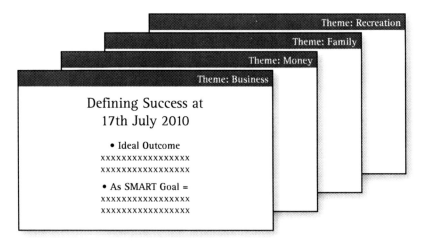

5. Look at the whole set together. Here are a couple of illustrative formats for presenting your required outcomes in a way that gives you the whole picture and further raises your motivation to

achieve it. These are just examples; choose one of them or create your own format to work for you.

(a) Outcome Statement – Tabular form

My Outcome Report 17ᵗʰ July 2010

Business Profile:

Successful high profile Chief Executive and biggest individual shareholder of Venture Capital backed alternative fuels business with resources and momentum to become industry leader in xxx sector across Europe.

Has increased equity value from £20 million to £150 million in past 3 years, established product leadership and UK distribution network. Full team of executives in place with equity incentives.

Chairman of UK Alternative Fuels Association, UK representative on European Council and member of government Working Party. A frequent speaker at industry events and Environmental Conferences.

Personal Outcomes	Personal State
• Hold target level of total/secure personal assets	Fulfilled
	Confident
• Regular 'B' team squash player.	
• Attended 6 R&B concerts in past year	Secure
• Travelled to 2 new places in past 12 months / 2 booked for next year	Civilised
	Progressing
• Spent 2 hours per week on personal reading	Winning
• Etc., etc.	Giving
	Learning
	Teaching
	Respecting
	Respected

(b) Outcome Statement – Storyboard form

Study your Consolidated Outcome Statement; leave it and go away to do something else; come back to look again. Allow at least 24 hours and perhaps up to a few weeks to move from your first draft through to total acceptance of your Outcome Statement before moving to the next stage.

Does the total picture and its components stack up? What would make life ideal at that time that you have not included?

6. Now write down how what you would have to do to achieve each outcome in strategic terms i.e. meaningful and precise but not too detailed.

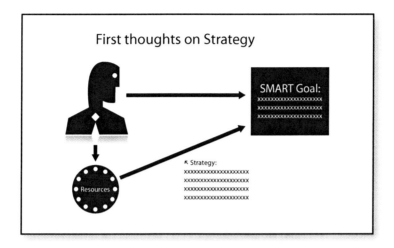

7. Again, look at the whole package across all your themes. Are the strategies compatible in time and other resources required, and with one another?

    If not, revise even the strategy or if that cannot be done go back to modify the goals – this time to achieve feasibility. In these circumstances, you have to choose between two or more outcomes that you desire but which cannot all be achieved.

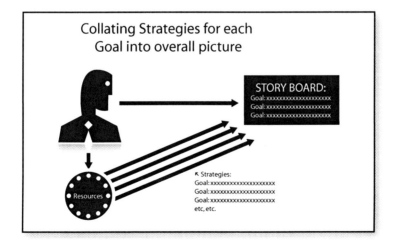

8. Your outcomes and the broad paths to arrive at them are now set. It is time to convert strategies into practical specific Work Plans.

    Become quite short term and very specific about the early stages of each strategy. It's helpful but not essential to have the same duration for each element. Continue your iterative checking for complete alignment.

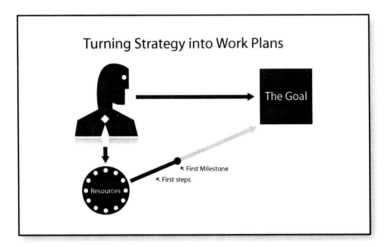

9. Prepare another snapshot view part way towards your longer term outcomes. For example, if you have developed an ideal set of outcomes for three years out then a one year interim picture could well be most appropriate.

    For your selected date, write your outcomes at that stage which will include the results of partially executed strategies. How does that look? Does it have your approval and belief in all respects? If not, why not? Put right.

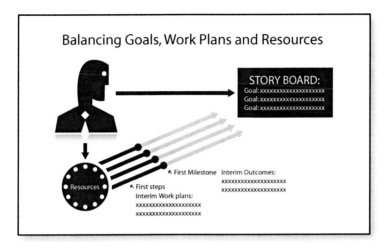

Balancing Goals, Work Plans and Resources

10. Now, move on from your analysis and planning into implementation. What will you complete in the next 7 days to take you satisfactorily towards your first Milestone outcomes? Write down and use as your time allocation and work plan for the coming week.

Why weekly? This short natural time frame ensures immediacy, should be easy to plan, encourages your early action and as the weeks go by demonstrates that you can and do succeed in your short goals and that you are making measurable progress towards your longer term outcomes.

Deciding on and Committing to Very First Steps

Weekly Report to 22nd July 2007

Business:
Book September flight to Australia
Fix J. Smith interview

Health and Fitness:
Make appointment with personal trainer. 3 x 2 miles jogs

Family:
Go to School Sports Day
Ask spouse to chose ideal day out together in next 4 weeks

Personal growth (Intellectual/Cultural)
Spend 3 x 45 minute sessions reading 'XYZ'

Other key actions:
Fill in tax return

11. Achieve what you promise yourself by the end of the week and repeat process until you meet your goals.

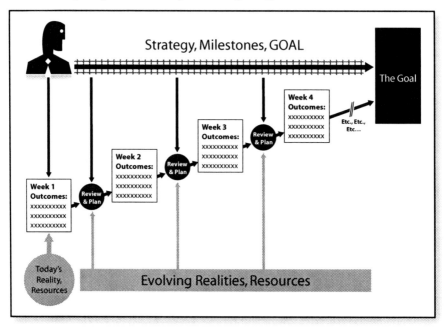

Does it sound simple? It is.

Does it sound very disciplined? It is, but that should not equate to bearing mechanical or anything less than enjoyable and fulfilling. Do build in 'buffers' of contingency time to accommodate the unscheduled events that affect everyone's weeks. Allow room for both planned and spontaneous enjoyment time.

Take time off from this regime in your holidays and similar periods. Even in working weeks, I find that sometimes taking a week off is refreshing and re-motivates me to return to it the following week. This process is intended to support you as a human – not turn you into a robot.

The reviews and the whole process should normally be enjoyable. If that is not the case with any frequency, it is very likely that there is misalignment somewhere within your plan. Discontent would then be a useful symptom to prompt you to re-examine your goals and your strategy, internal and external realities and your time allocation and management.

At all stages, including the weekly review, it is really helpful to have a buddy, whether a paid professional or just as a friend, to be your sounding board. We will look at that option shortly.

6.2 How to Get What You DON'T Want

Don't change anything,

just carry on as you are.

So far, little mention has been made of how to select your strategy in either the leadership processes described in Chapter 5 or in the context of preparing your Personal Business Plan in Chapter 6.1 above. That omission is intentional and appropriate for the content of your strategy will be as individual as you are. If required, there are many sources of guidance to strategy setting covering all aspects from business logic and objective decision making tools through to developing productive and creative planning teams.

As an exception to the general stance, I will mention one valuable tool that can contribute a great deal to both forming a strategy and subsequently implementing it. It is an appropriate exception, for it is the opposite of 'how to?'. It is 'how not to?' and, apparently the converse of the positive thinking about goals otherwise associated with *The Effective Entrepreneur*.

Strangely, asking such questions such as 'How would we not achieve our goal?", "What could get in the way of our Strategy?" can be very revealing, useful and positive.

Furthermore, looking at potential obstacles accords with two principal themes of *The Effective Entrepreneur*. By looking for threats and what could go wrong, we are temporarily changing our view of the world. We are changing our perspective by looking at our strategy, our goal and our context differently.

Our search for danger will entail looking out onto the landscape to identify potential obstacles standing between us and our goal, with special attention to those nearest our chosen path. In business, that landscape is normally dynamic rather than static. To understand latent threats, we may want to assume the position of another party such as a prospective customer or a competitor to understand the world from their viewpoint. That will necessitate looking back in on ourselves, a very healthy perspective when done with true empathy with that other party [36].

Inhibitors to success can arise from inside us and our team as well as out there in the landscape. An objective assessment of our abilities and our innermost concerns often reveals another category of risk to our stated ambitions.

---

36 An opportunity to practice Perceptual Positioning (see page 36).

Reference to ourselves and our readiness to take the necessary actions becomes even more relevant as the planning phase draws to a close and implementation looms large. Reluctance to take action or even to settle on the strategy itself, a particular form of prevarication, is every bit as great a danger to accomplishment as any difficulty in forming the right strategy. In fact, for the population at large it may well be the most frequent reason that dreams do not materialise.

When an impediment arises from inner doubts or finding the time to start an activity, a personal coach is often the most effective resource to move from good, but unexecuted, intentions to a 100% motivation and commitment to take those first steps that remove major problems and/or put your long term strategy into action.

'Set the Goal, Form a Strategy, Remove the Impediments' is an obvious simplification of real life but one that has merit as a leader's mantra. After all, if the required destination is known and there is energy applied in the direction of achieving the goal, if there is no resistance or impediment then the goal must be reached.

A variation of our temporary 'why won't it work?' approach is posing questions like "What happens if I do nothing?", "What will be the results of continuing as we are?" and "This [sales person] has underperformed for the past 3 years, why will next year be different?" The challenge to the *status quo* or to the implicit assumptions underlying our plans keeps us vigilant against lazy or wishful thinking.

When the question relates to evidence such as the "why will next year be different?" or "why should somebody buy from us?" an honest answer often replaces false or empty optimism. Positive thinking and optimism are great assets of a good leader but must be based on reality to maximise the probability of a successful outcome and keep credibility with one's team.

A LITLE HELP FROM
YOUR FRIENDS

7.1 Your Team

Provided that your aspirations stretch beyond the capacity of you to do everything in your business, you are going to need other people to help you. The quality of your choices and means to keep them fully motivated to your cause is therefore vital to you success.

The team of people that report to you directly is particularly important. The Bibliography includes sample sources from an extensive range of literature about team building. The following comments are restricted to identifying the purpose for you in having a team and key comments about each reason.

The first reason is simply one of **capacity**. Effective managers extend the level of business that you can handle. The key requirement is for them to execute that work reliably and largely self sufficiently to the standard that you require. You do not need people to micro manage.

Secondly, you probably need specialist capability, or **expertise** beyond merely the capacity to replicate your skills. The capability may be in any area of your business. Finance, Sales, Engineering, Operations management would be typical functional capabilities where again you want self sufficient people to reliably handle a part of your business, this time beyond the level that you could achieve yourself. Again, they should not need close management but they do need leading. They must understand your Goal, your overall strategy and what role you expect them to play.

In today's fast moving knowledge-based economy, the notion that the leader is the only source of ideas, which are then handed down for others to execute is long dead. You want a team that will contribute **ideas** and filter and convert into executable strategies within your overall direction. At this stage, the concept of a diverse yet coherent group of individuals forming a team becomes important for a mix of different personality types is most conducive to effectiveness in this area[37].

Finally, on the basis that we are all human, your team will both need and offer mutual **personal support**, camaraderie and the means to sustain motivation. For this reason too, the mix of people recruited into your team is vital.

---

[37] R. Meredith Belbin, *Team Roles at Work*, (Butterworth-Heinemann 1993)

As you move forward, the landscape in which your team is expected to perform will change and over time, team members may change too. It is current and future **performance** that matter to you. Ensure that you can objectively expect each team member to play their full part in the next stage of your journey. If your Goal matters, pursuing it effectively must be the sole reason for retaining each individual. That can be a tough standard to act upon on in a small company but if you do not, you are giving yourself a handicap and indicating that something else is more important than the health of your business.

7.2 Your Personal Business Coach

In the very early days of a business, it may be possible for the leader to be 'one of the crowd' with a start up team of cornerstone colleagues. This is often a highly fun phase with everyone clubbing in together and doing whatever needs doing with you as the lead doer. In this atmosphere of close proximity and high informality, it is entirely appropriate to finish the day with a drink together at the pub or wine bar.

However, at some stage you will have to make decisions that need to be objective, may not be popular and may be bad news for some of your colleagues/friends. Start ups that grow almost invariably find that some of the starting team struggle as the business grows. The cause may be a lack of competence or discomfort with the constraints of more structure and process. What do you do about that drag on your performance? It is an important decision; a telling fork in your road with the stark choices being friendship or performance. From a business perspective, many entrepreneurs hold back their companies by loyally staying with their original team too long.

The Effective Entrepreneur does assume the responsibility for the final word and ultimate accountability. However, smart and capable team members may be, Leadership is a specific role and a business or a project only has room for one leader[38].

[38] That statement is not to be confused with your team being as smart and capable as possible or taking all the help available. Jack Welch was succinct in the former respect when he said "If you [as leader] are the smartest guy in the team you're a jackass" was his version of this truth.

Lesson: Finding an appropriate Distance between Leader and Led

My Chairman told me that I had got too far ahead of my team – and it was not a compliment.

In my enthusiasm to keep pressing ahead, I had not listened to key members of my management team who, at heart, didn't share my ambition and would have settled for a quieter well paid life at 'cruising height' rather than continuing to ascend (sensible chaps!).

Because I was so much in evangelising mode thinking I was motivating them - and they didn't tell me anything different (people don't) – I didn't read the signs and so when the going got tough they were not 'the tough to get going'.

I would have done much better to have recognise the need to have changed and upgraded the team when we were playing strongly in better times.

From that experience, I conceptualised the positioning of a leader as a pacemaker on an athletics track. The required outcome is to achieve a specified 'stretch' target in the form of a world record. If the pacemaker is in with the pack, he/she is doing no good in terms of pulling performance beyond the ordinary or comfortable. If he/she runs too far ahead, the 'pull factor' is broken and the leader becomes irrelevant to the team from which the record holder should emerge. Setting an appropriate pace with the right distance between pacemaker and pack, means that it is essential to monitor the clock and the on track position of the runners, if the right result is to be attained. That is a useful image for me.

We never attempted to take this analogy though to the point that the pacemaker becomes irrelevant and drops out. Perhaps one should!

The leader is out on his/her own. It is a very rare person that does not sometimes agree that 'it can be lonely at the top'. Toughing it out does not, in its own right, win prizes – which can lead to a blinkered approach with available help being rejected.

There are occasions when 'two heads are better than one'. For the independent leader, another person to test ideas with is a great advantage.

The 'second head' should ensure that an 'outside looking in' or 'top of the tree' perspective is taken up. That facility alone is invaluable for the leader who knows his/her goal and resources intimately and finds it difficult to step above the detail. Adding an appropriate view of the terrain to be covered facilitates good and timely decision making.

It is also healthy to recognise that an appropriate confidante is a source of boosting one's own morale and motivation from time to time. Those positive feelings uplift business effectiveness. The personal benefit is often interwoven with talking out a problematic situation until a satisfactory strategy is reached. Whether the starting point for that discussion is business or personal is immaterial, for everything must be brought together and aligned for confidence to be in place.

Gaining 100% confidence that you are doing the right thing is the immovable and magic criterion. Meeting this standard is the result of satisfying both all your objective thoughts and sub conscious feelings, so it is the best possible test that you have the right answer. Once achieved, a leader's 100% confidence is then a major causal factor of success – and any shortfall, a major cause of failure[39].

It is imperative that the 'second head' is unambiguously and exclusively in support of you and works in complete confidence. The exclusive motivation must be to further your interests; there must no other agenda. Any deviation from this role must inhibit your freedom to share thoughts and thus reduces the chances of finding the best answers. For this reason your confidante cannot be a colleague or your manager. Even Non Executive Directors and Chairmen may carry too much of an 'agenda' from their formal responsibilities and possibly sectional interests such as representing a Venture Capitalist.

Lesson: Why Line Managers and Boardroom colleagues cannot be your personal Coach.

Even in the best Chairman – CEO relationships it probably remains difficult for the CEO to 'front up', to express his doubts that he will hit his numbers or does not feel confident about handling particular situations.

---

[39] Remember, Successful People Act 'As If' (see page 42)

Still more, in a formal relationship it is not easy to be entirely open about personal matters that impinge on business. A coaching client of mine confided that he knew he needed to put a lot of personal time to ensure that a planned development in South America would be successful. He also knew that his wife, fed up with being left at home with their young children, had told him, 'one more weekend away this year and you'll have to choose between the job and me'. How would my client approach that situation with his Chairman?

Most of us have some concerns like this at some time and I would be surprised if I was alone in keeping too many of them entirely to myself in the past. How much better it would be if you could share the entire picture with a suitable person entirely on your side.

I have used a personal coach for the past four years and benefited enormously. I just wish that I had understood coaching and employed one in the frenetic and sometimes tough years when I was a Chief Executive.

The following summary of what Coaching is about:

Coaching

Coaching is a method of facilitating another person's learning, development and performance.

Through coaching people:

* Find their own solutions

* Develop their own skills

* Change their own behaviours

* Change their own attitudes

* Access their own inner wisdom

The Coach's Role is to enable the individual to identify blind spots with the sole objective of helping them to draw on whatever resources are needed to raise their performance to their required levels. Without coaching, people continue to merely hone their existing level of performance.

This role is Differentiated from others by recognition of the following:

Trainer – deals with input of knowledge and skill

Mentor – an industry or subject matter expert who recommends a course to follow on a continuing basis

Consultant - an expert who diagnoses and recommends solutions to specific issues according to brief

Executive – sets direction, manages processes and performance

Counsellor – helps people without the strength of inner resource to do so themselves. Remedial in nature

Coach – helps people achieve their gaols by using their own inner resources; focuses on the future.

The Skills of a Coach are:

* The ability to build rapport and offer the best setting for a client to be totally frank

* Good questions to enable the client to fully discover own thoughts and feelings

* Great use of all of own senses to understand client's degree of congruity with answers given and conclusions reached (known as sensory acuity).

* Use of Goal and Strategy setting techniques

* Eliciting motivation for client to take required actions

* Corrective Interventions when the client is displaying incongruence of any sort, attitudes or beliefs that are inhibiting performance and/or not taking agreed actions.

At the **core of Coaching is a goals driven, mutually agreed and committed partnership,** in which the coach's intention is to empower, facilitate and enable the individual to exceed prior levels of personal and professional performance. The coach supports the client to find their

> own solutions, develop their skills and knowledge and modify their behaviours and attitudes to address their chosen goals.

Like their sporting counterparts, business coaches cannot step over the line to participate themselves. The relationship and time spent is for the client, not the coach. A coach can only achieve success through the client's performance.

Coaching is a very personal business. Never appoint a coach without at least one meaningful meeting and a satisfactory personal 'chemistry test'. In this context just go with how you feel; there is no need to rationalise any negative decision.

Review any appointment periodically and be ready to change as soon as that would be better for you. Perhaps, unlike any other relationship, the only thing that matters in a coaching relationship is that it is effective for you.

Just as no Olympic athlete would contemplate pursuit of a gold medal without a coach, be ready to make the equivalent investment in your world class business performance.

CONCLUSION

8. CONCLUSION

The intention of *The Effective Entrepreneur* has been to offer practical guidance about how "how to run a successful business" and how to align it with a fulfilling personal life. For many of us, knowing how to realise those outcomes would have considerable value.

The Core Skills and Processes (Chapter 5) and Your Personal Business Plan (Chapter 6) offer specific methodologies, which provide:

- the opportunity to review and upgrade basic fundamentals which we all do but may not have stopped to make explicit to ourselves and people we work with.

   Through active consideration, adopting consistent ways to lead and manage, and spelling them out to colleagues, we can significantly uplift performance, not least through greatly improved communications, arguably the most common inhibitor of effective team working.

- an invaluable point of reference when the going is tough and real life seems unstructured or confusing. In these circumstances, revisiting the roadmap offered by *The Effective Entrepreneur* can be the means to regroup, restore order and return to a proven professional process for moving forward.

Those central ideas should be set in the context of the whole path of *The Effective Entrepreneur* which has been to:

- identify you and what singles you out from the crowd;

- underline the importance of a clear goal, with which you totally identify, and a strategy to achieve it which you are convinced you are able to carry out;

- alert you to the necessity of being able to stand outside your immediate situation to see the relationship of where you are now, your goal and the landscape that needs to be negotiated to take you to it.

Such an appropriate perspective allows you to confirm or alter your route i.e. your strategy. Seeing the route to your attainable goal should also motivate you to take the first steps along the optimum path, rather than any other direction or inaction.

- offer you the opportunity to learn through reflection against my entrepreneurial history (both as I interpret the learning points and as you discern for yourself);

- synthesise all my experience into a framework that gives you a secure foundation to be an effective leader and manager. It comprises:

  - an explicit core process of <u>goal setting, delegation and monitoring</u>

  - a guide for ensuring <u>alignment of internal and external factors</u> in your business from the most helpful perspective

  - <u>a step-by-step method</u> for setting up and maintaining your <u>self leadership and self management</u> to attain your ideal personal outcomes, with specific recommendations that:

    - you select your goals from a comprehensive set of all possible elements of your completely ideal destination thus ensuring that your <u>Personal Business Plan</u> includes everything that you wish to achieve

    - you recognise the need to attain <u>personal satisfaction as you travel</u> towards your goals as well as on their achievement – and include the means to attain it in your strategy

  - identifying the <u>impediments</u> to your success and prioritising their <u>removal</u>

  - emphasising the merits of seeking <u>appropriate help from others</u> to maximise your effectiveness. There are no prizes for shouldering the entire burden yourself and you are likely to be less effective if you try. On various appropriate bases, others want to help you. I specifically recommend appointing your own personal coach.

You may recall that I set myself the challenge of writing down something 'coherent, practical and comprehensive' to help you and me as independent business leaders. The case for coherence and practicality will stand or fall by what you have read so far.

The search for comprehensiveness requires a little more examination. I have come to realise that any notion of completeness can only apply in the sense that the above framework can accommodate all the more detailed techniques and content necessary for your journey.

Drilling down to a lower level would be counter productive if the brevity needed for practicality is to be maintained. Pursuit of complete answers of greater granularity could be a barrier to effectiveness. You already have enough knowledge to be successful. The real enabler of success is actually taking the first step on your journey not just wondering what or when it will be. *The Effective Entrepreneur* gives you the resources to identify and implement that right first step and beyond.

Universality would have been a more appropriate aim than comprehensiveness and one that is, I believe, achieved by *The Effective Entrepreneur.*

With your own interpretation of the methods I have described, you have more than enough knowledge to succeed in leading and managing yourself and others on your entrepreneurial journey. When you add your drive and that unique 'something special' you will enjoy great success.

Unless you change something that you currently do, any existing shortfall in performance and satisfaction will remain unchanged. If you do not change anything, you will not meet your aspirations and your frustration in underachieving can only increase.

When you adopt the practical methods of *The Effective Entrepreneur* you will discover your best set of personalised goals and feel good about the journey towards achieving them from now on.

I believe that my proposition, as repeated below, is well founded:

For readers fully engaging with it, this book gives hard working business leaders the opportunity to learn how to achieve full success in their business and personal lives. .... in good times and bad .... the ideas put forward are practical to implement.

So, I would again urge you to take the next step and produce a Personal Business Plan as described in Chapter 6 and carry on learning through every means at your disposal. When you take your first committed steps along this route, you are on the way to realising your ambitions and the ideal personal state to which you aspire.

Writing *The Effective Entrepreneur* has been a great learning process for me. I shall continue learning through future publications via my web site www.johncaines.com, the printed word and by personal delivery. I invite you to join me to share part of our respective journies.

I hope that *The Effective Entrepreneur* has already done good things for you and that it serves you well in your future.

Bibliography

Geoffrey Moore, *Crossing the Chasm*, (Harper Collins, 1991)*

Michael E Gerber, *E Myth Mastery*, (Harper Collins, 2005)

Catherine Benko and F. Warren McFarlan, *Connecting the Dots*, (Harvard Business School Press, 2003)

Jack Welch, Jack, (Warner Books Inc., 2001)*

Paul McKenna, *Instant Confidence* (Bantam Press, 2006)

Charles Handy, The Elephant and the Flea, (Random House, 2002)

Jim Collins, Good to *Great*, (Random house, 2001)*

Eliyahu M. Goldratt, *The Goal*, (North River Press, 2004)

Stephen R. Covey, *The 7 Habits of Highly Effective People*, (Fireside, 1989)

Joe O'Connor, *NLP Handbook*, (Thorsons, 2001)

R. Meredith Belbin, *Team Roles at Work*, (Butterworth-Heinemann 1993)

* These are publications that I found to be inspirational and with broad application for the business leader. (That statement implies no deficiency in the other titles; simply that they have addressed specific rather than universal issues for me).

www.johncaines.com will feature a recommended reading list with facility for others to provide feedback and add their own recommendations.

About the Author

John Caines is a Chairman, Investor and Business Coach who enables businesses and business people to achieve their goals following his own successful entrepreneurial career.

Disillusioned with corporate life at an early age, he took an MBA at London Business School before setting up his first business at 26. He developed two software and service companies before leading the Management Buy Out of an eight person business, which he turned, into a profitable £40 million p.a. group that is now quoted on the London AIM Stock Market. In the process, he raised private equity, started local operations in seven European countries and completed eleven company acquisition and disposal transactions.

After a successful exit from his main business in 2001, John turned to helping other business leaders, especially entrepreneurs through a portfolio of directorships, coaching and consulting assignments. He has led both company turnarounds and rapid growth situations. He has chaired a thriving Business Angel Network and personally invested in eighteen early stage companies over the past five years. As its Chairman, he repositioned one company to achieve a return of five times initial investment within a year when co-investing alongside a venture capitalist.

He is a frequent speaker at events for the entrepreneurial community on the subjects of business leadership and early stage business funding.

"Your method of integrating business and personal planning really struck home for me. I've told my board colleagues that we must read The Effective Entrepreneur from cover to cover and then use its ideas to communicate between ourselves in the future."

Managing Director, £8 million on line marketing company

"The blend of personal anecdote and specific methodologies in The Effective Entrepreneur reinforce one another make it an enjoyable read. I will find those methods a good practical framework to help me work with clients more effectively."

Business Coach

"John has helped me understand the CFO and the CFO understand me. We were more aligned in our goals than either of us had realised. We are now more productive than ever before".

Creative VP, $10 million consumer products company

Printed in the United Kingdom by
Lightning Source UK Ltd., Milton Keynes
137015UK00001B/55-81/A